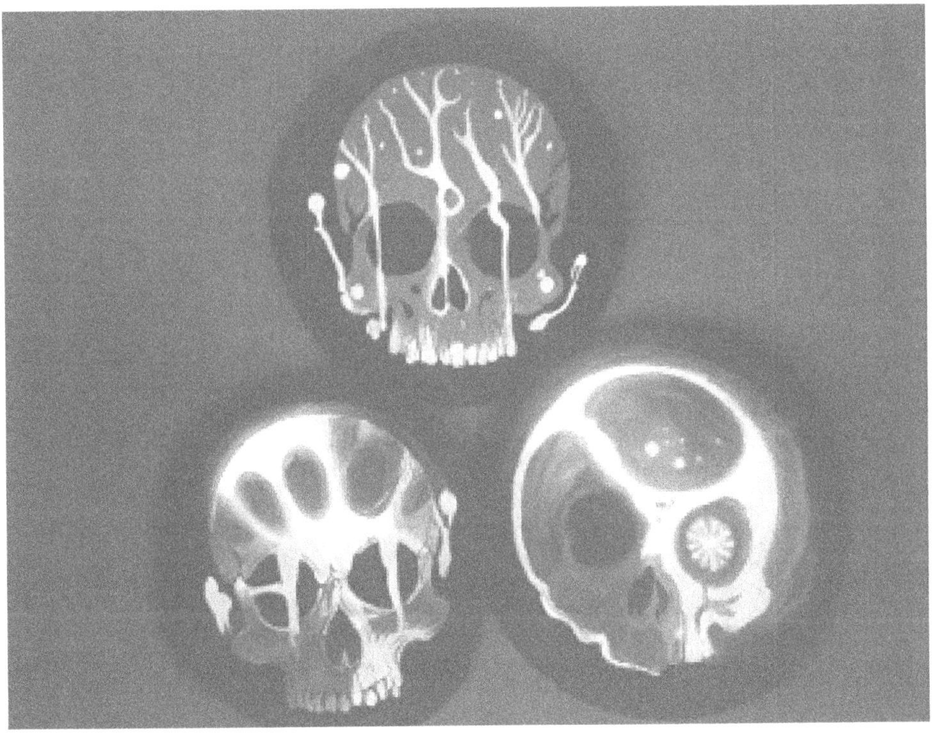

Tripping Hard or Hardly Tripping

JedidiahDrotar

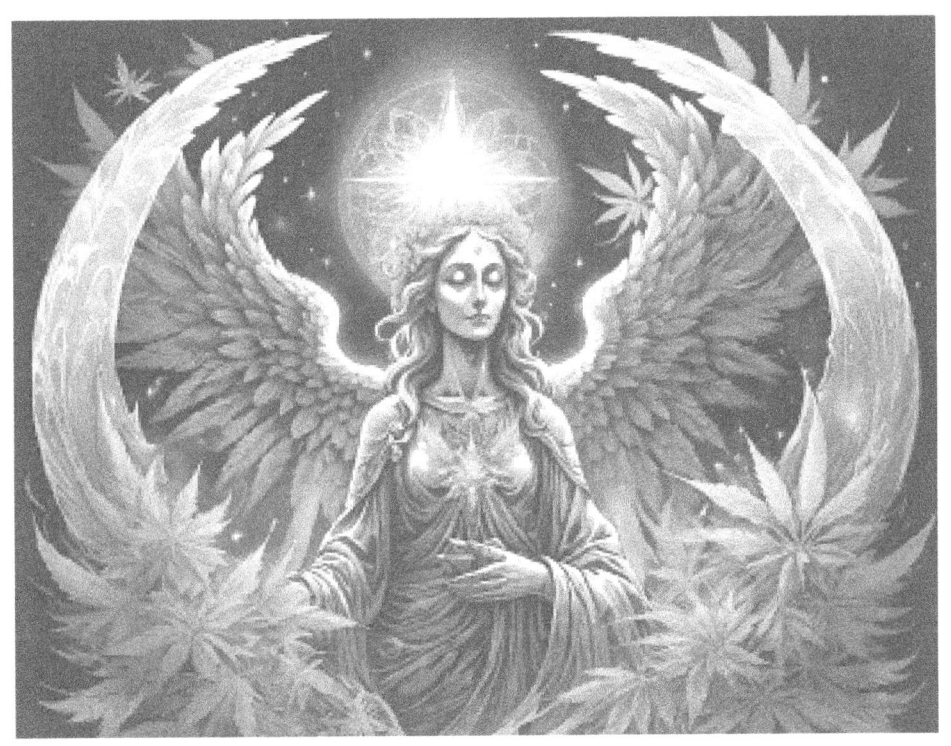

JedidiahDrotar

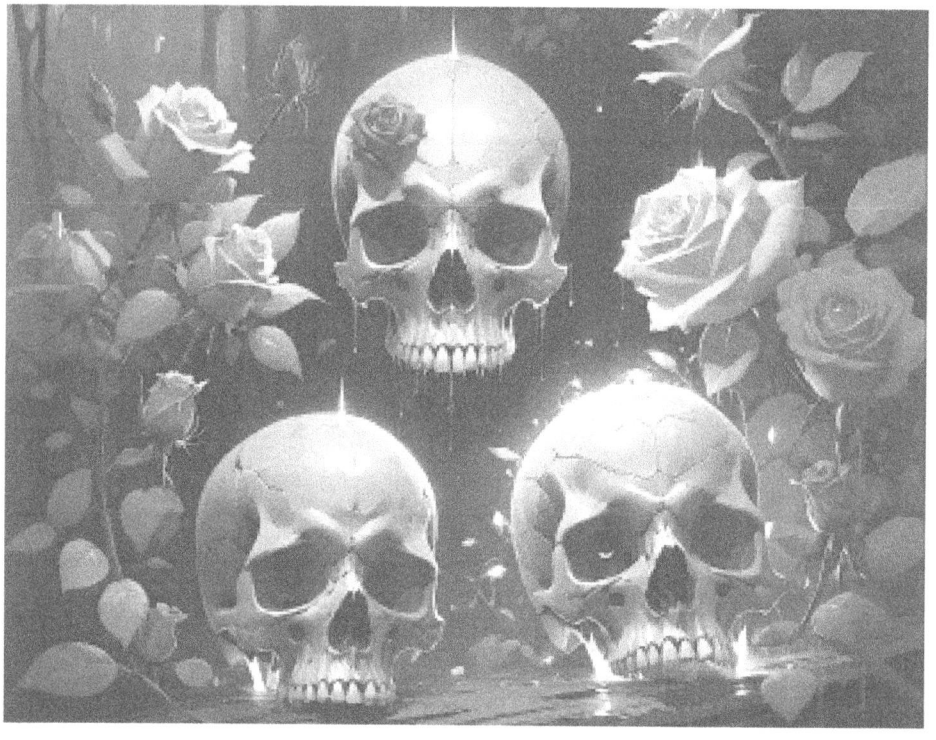

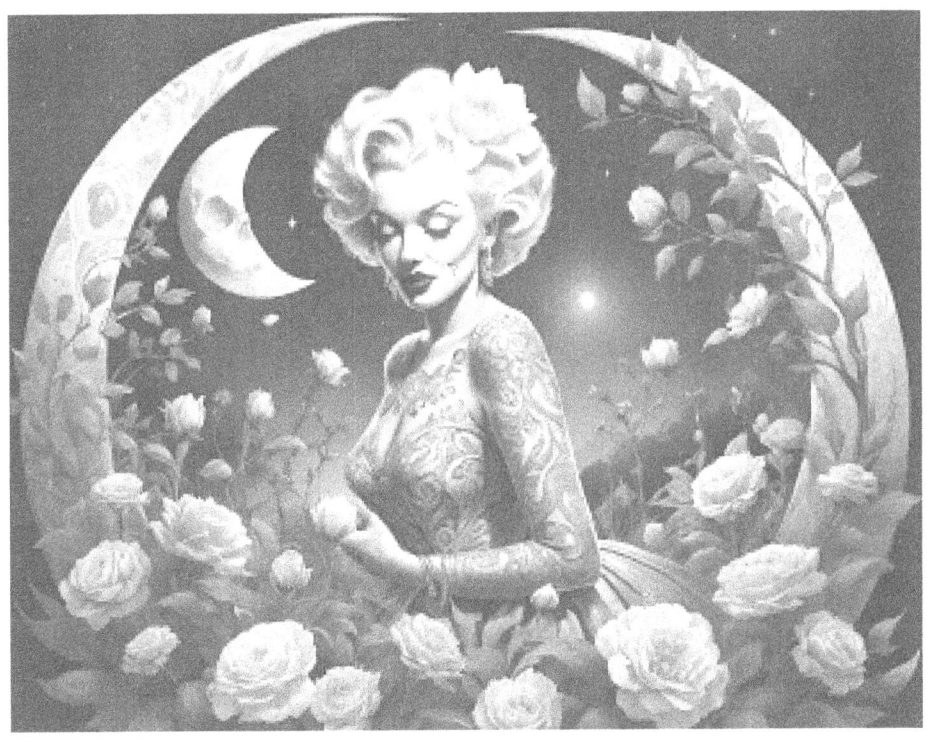

JedidiahDrotar

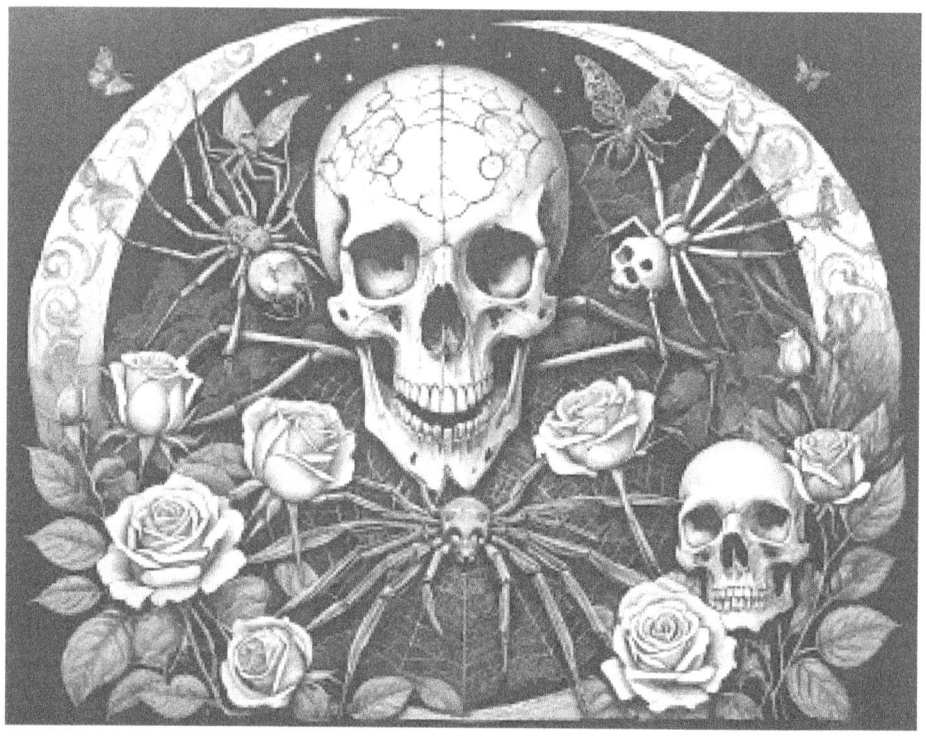

Tripping Hard or Hardly Tripping

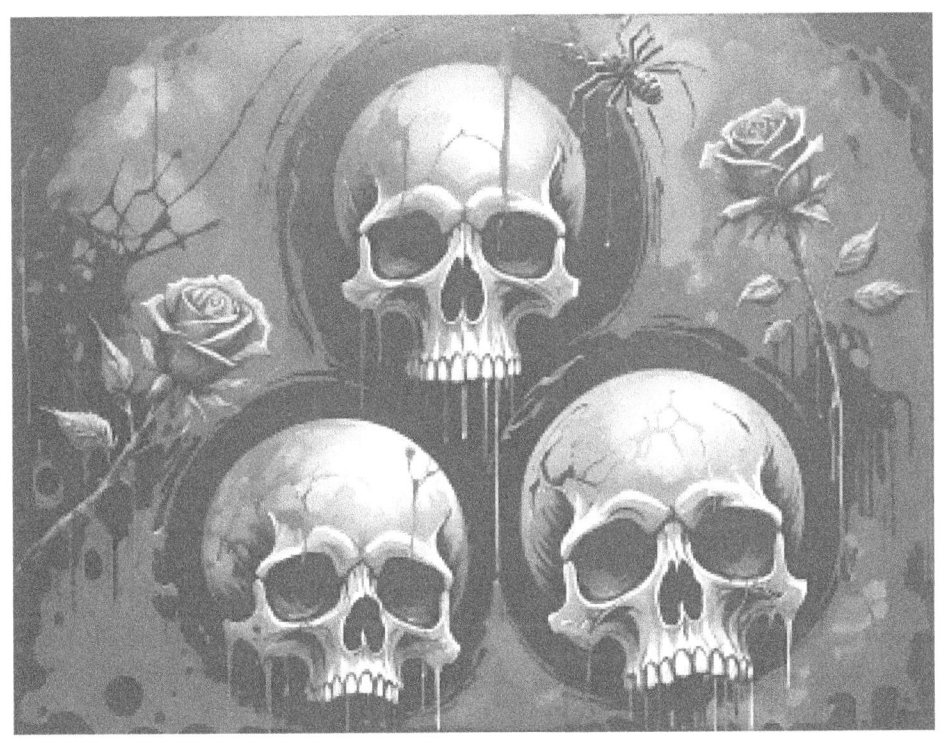

JedidiahDrotar

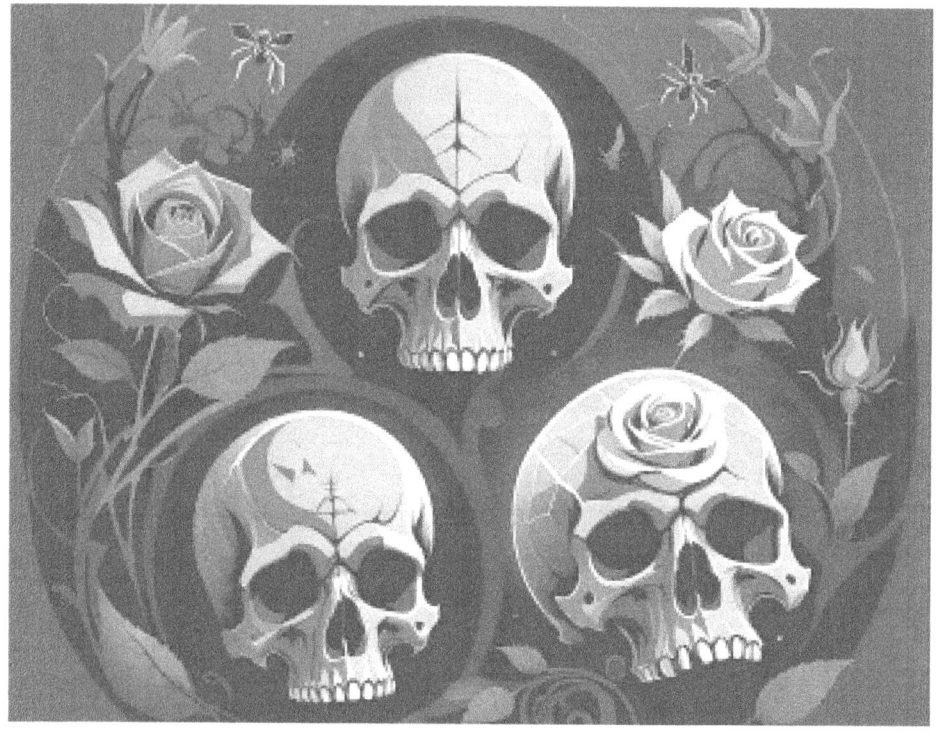

Tripping Hard or Hardly Tripping

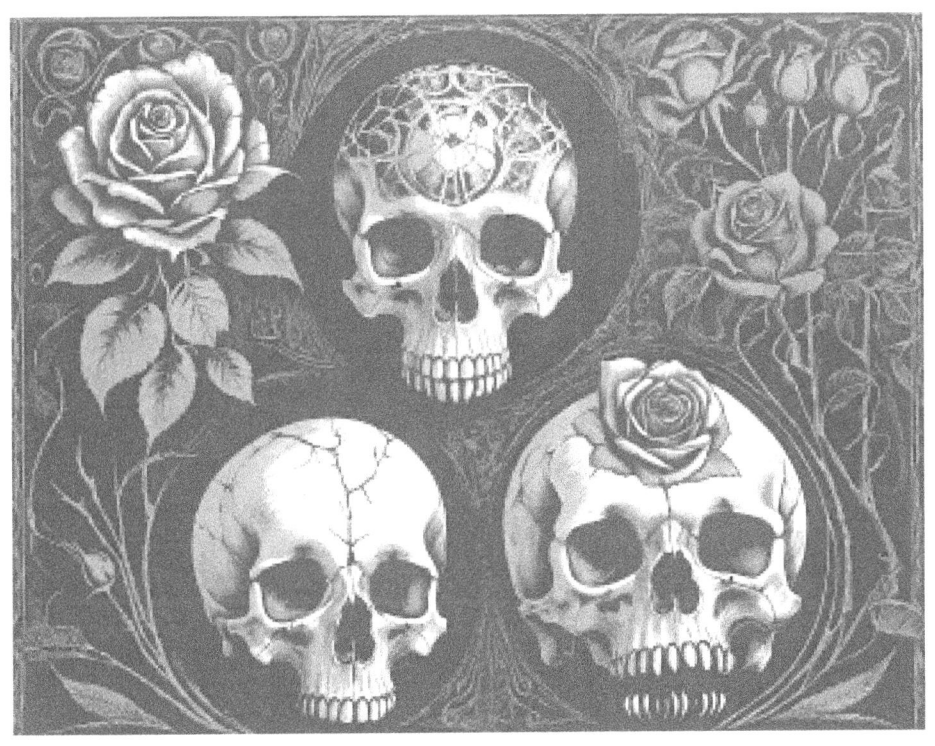

JedidiahDrotar

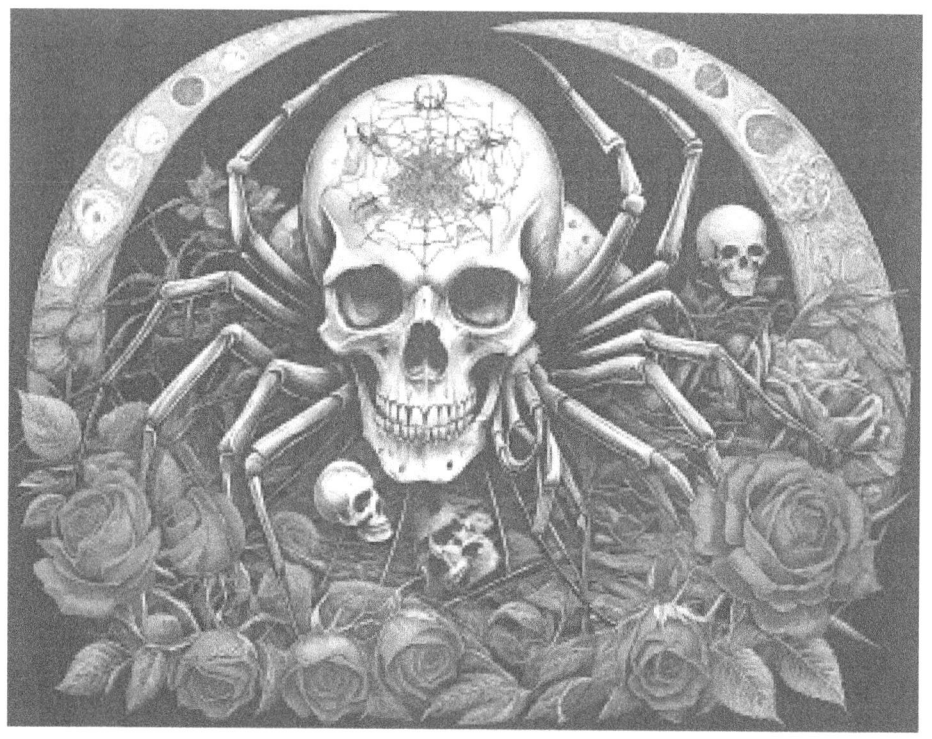

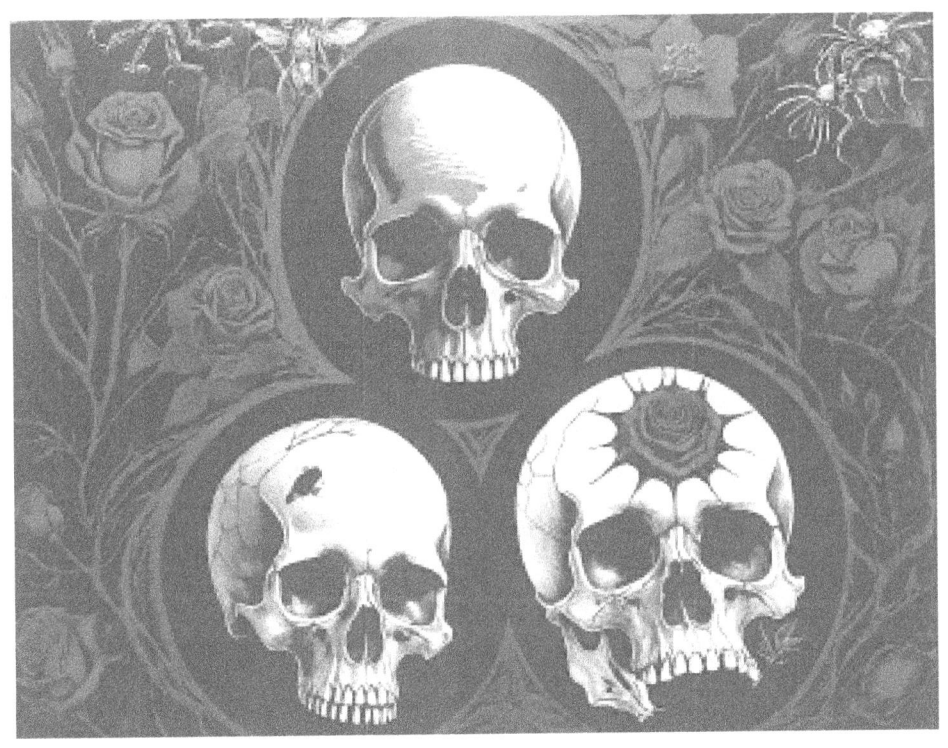

JedidiahDrotar

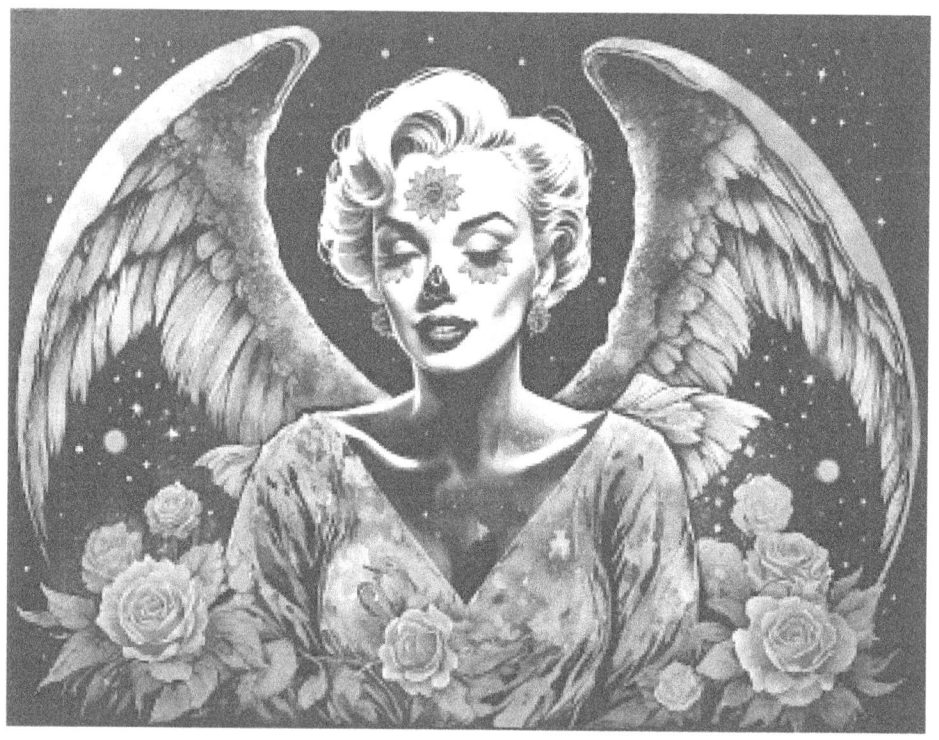

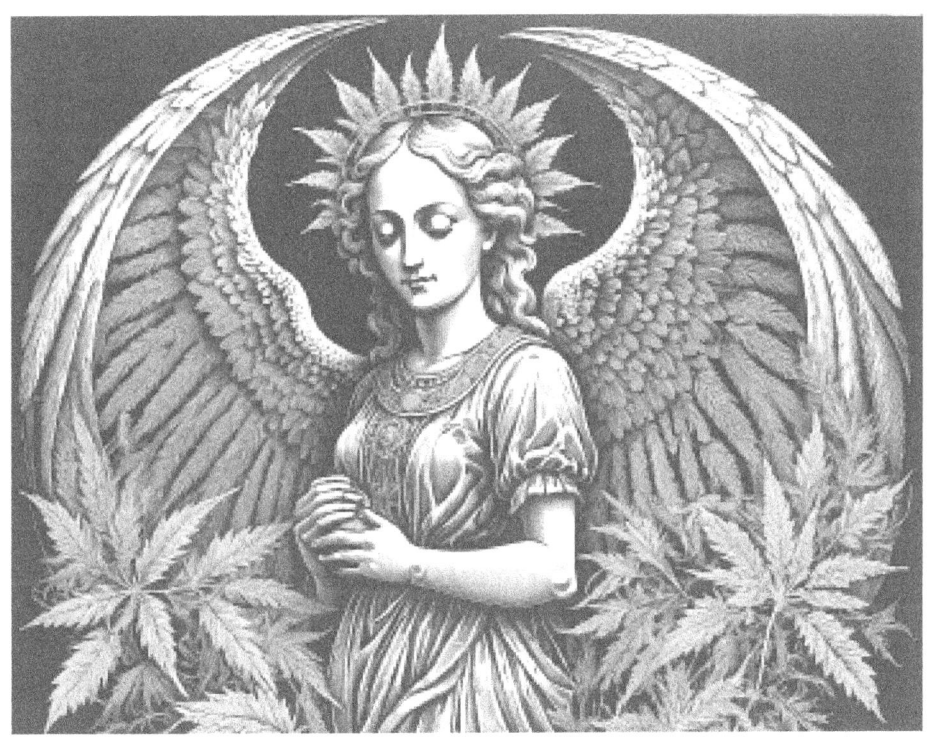

JedidiahDrotar

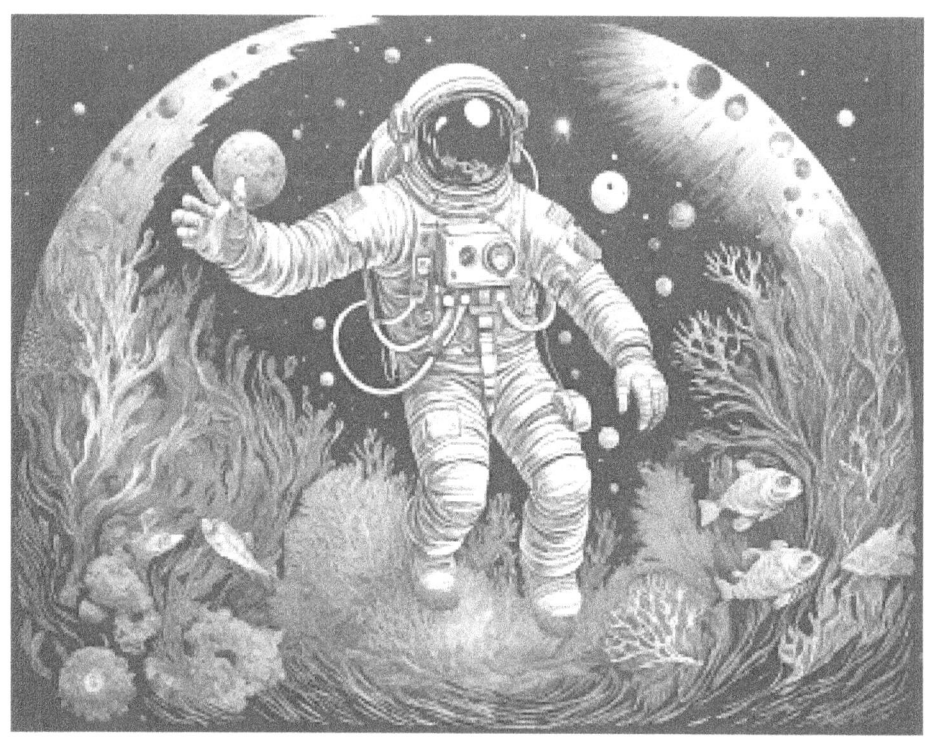

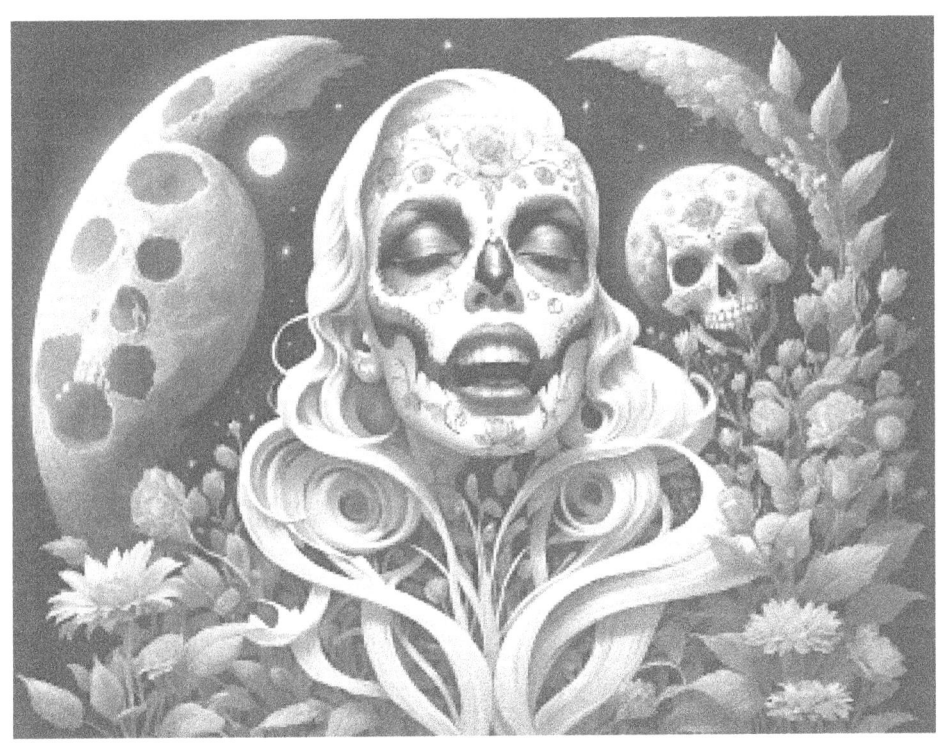

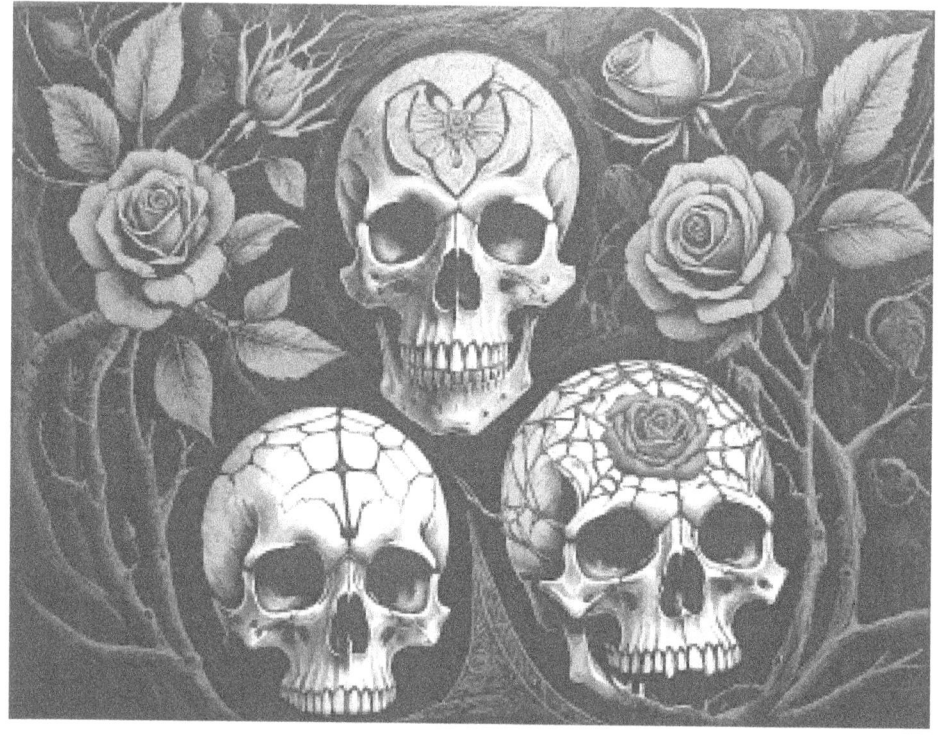

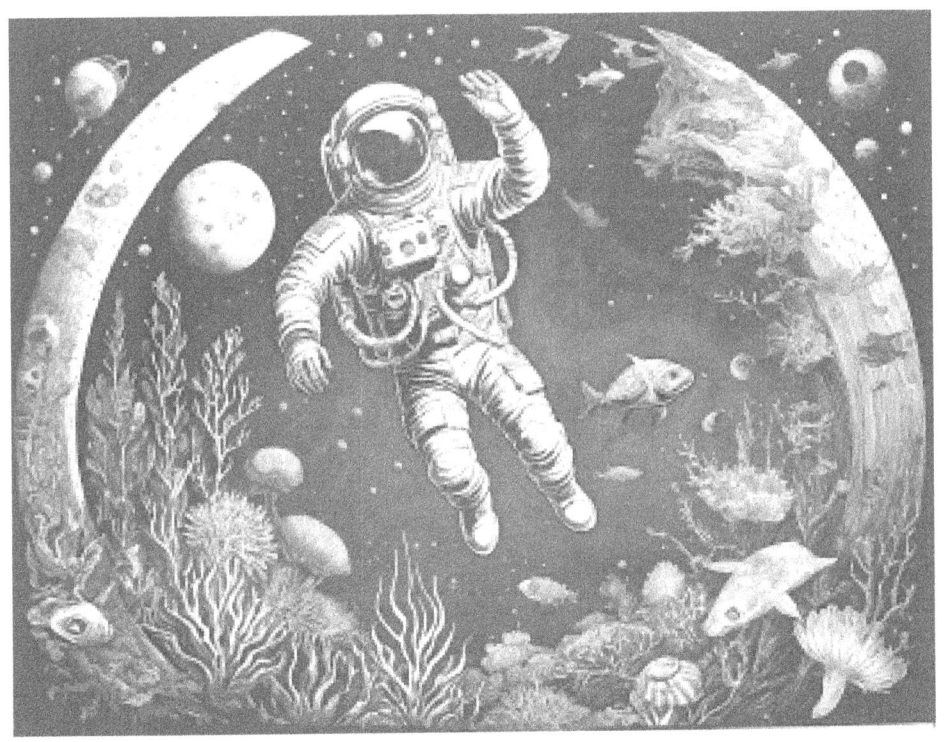

JedidiahDrotar

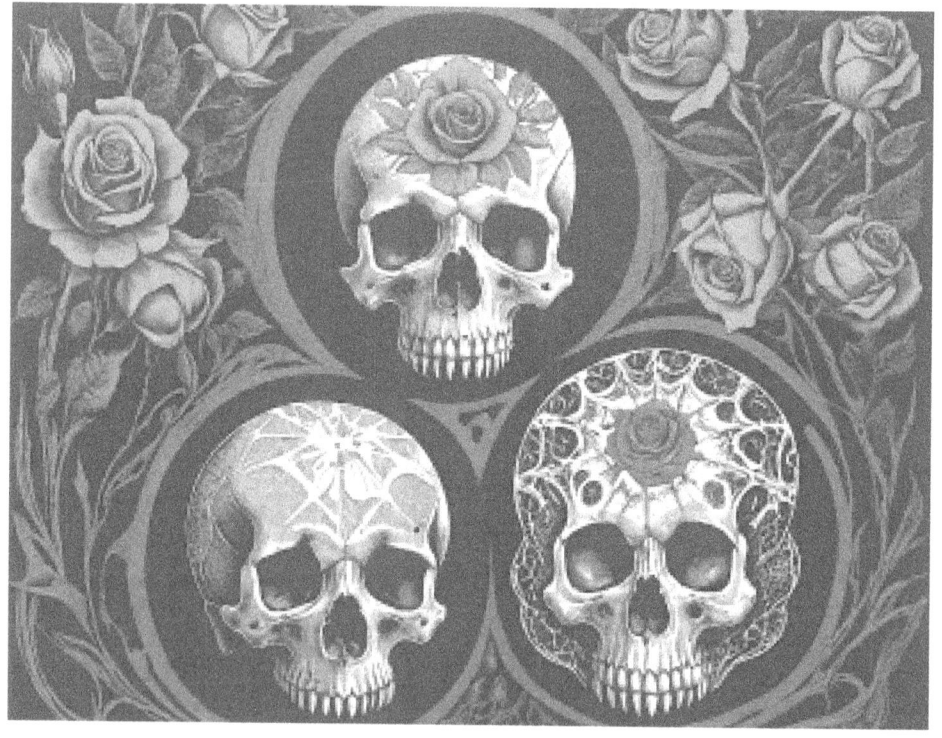

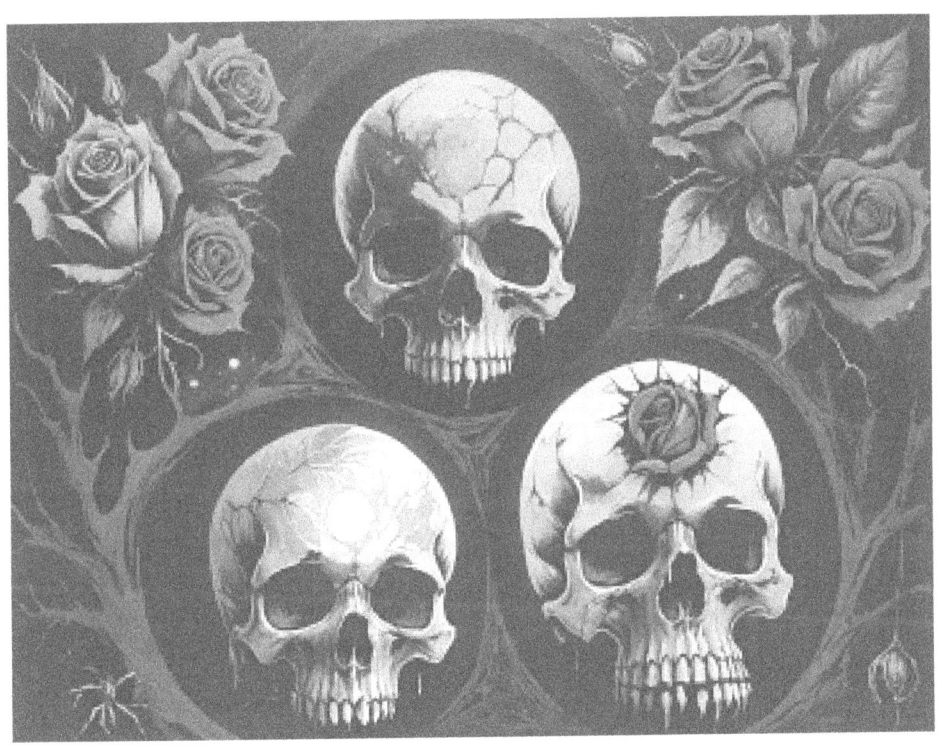

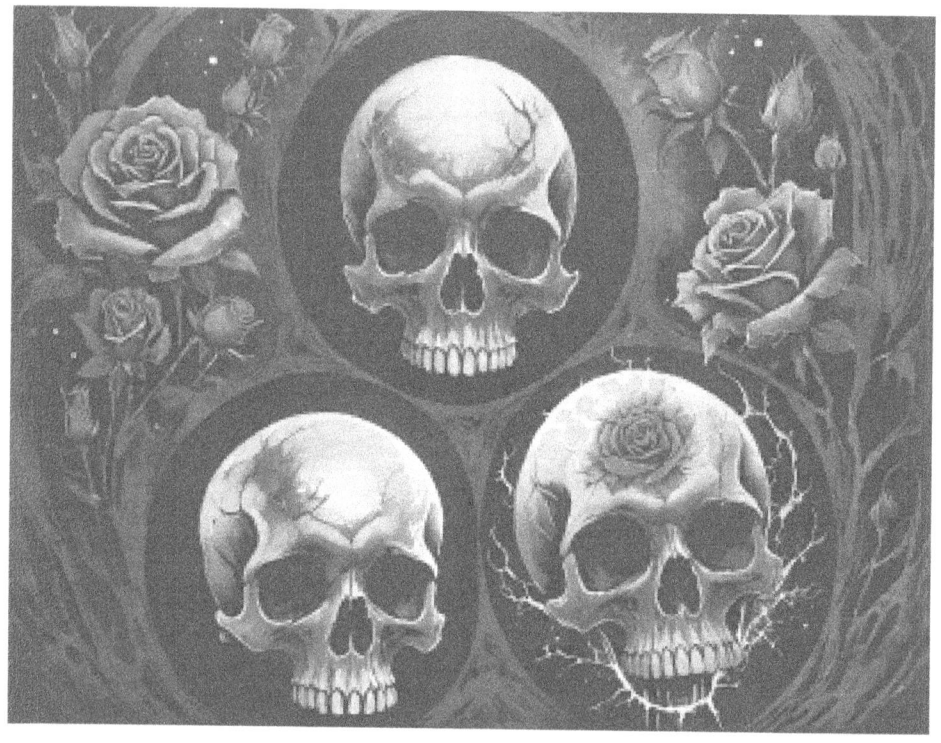

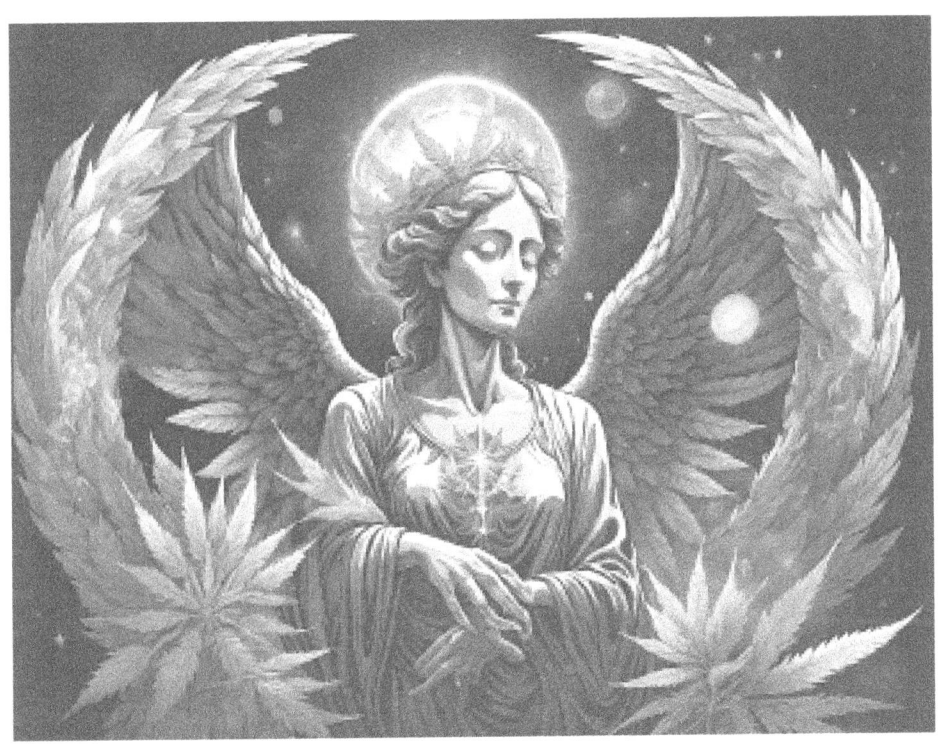

JedidiahDrotar

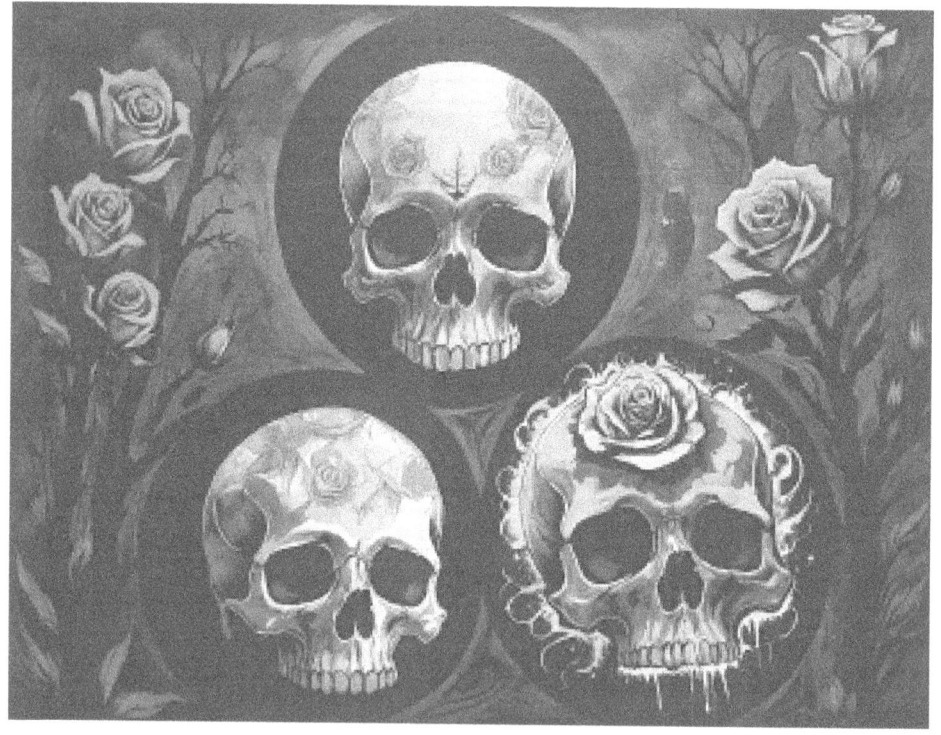

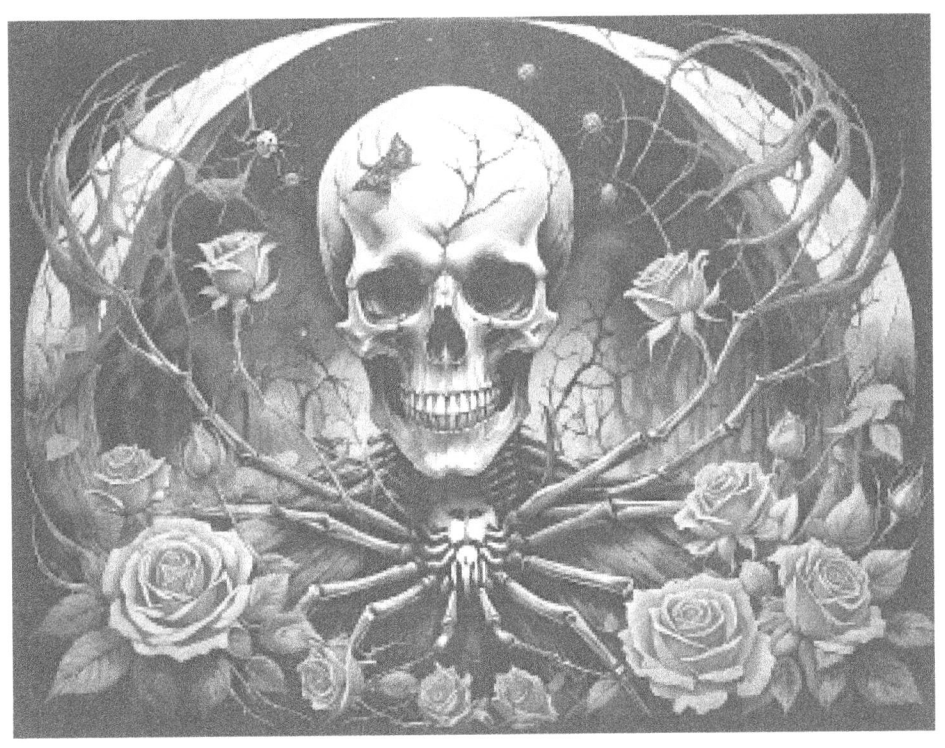

JedidiahDrotar

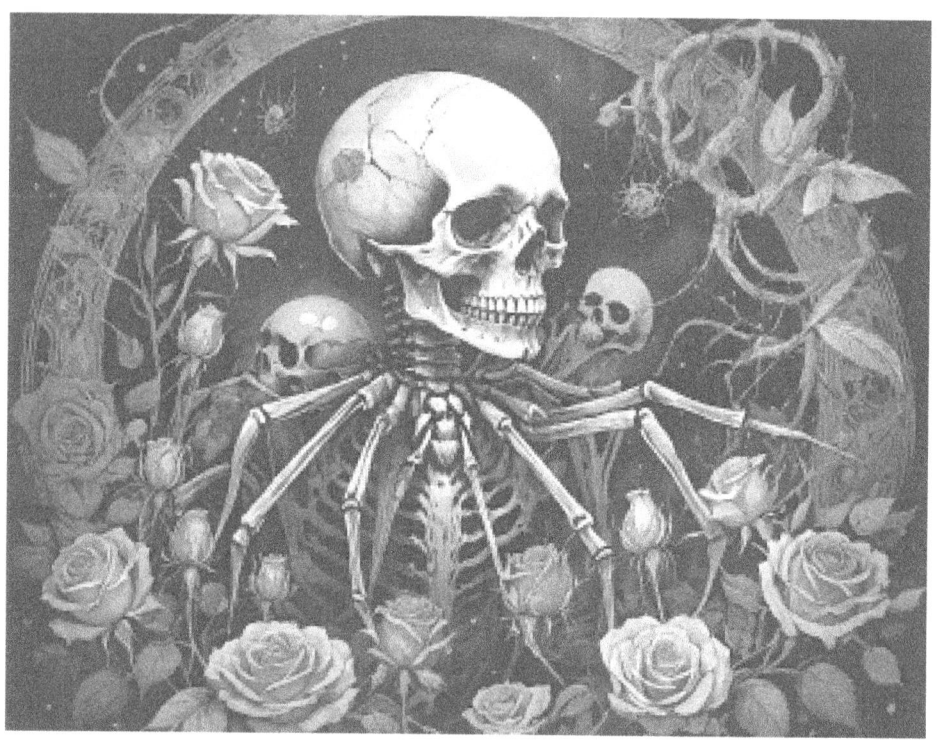

Tripping Hard or Hardly Tripping

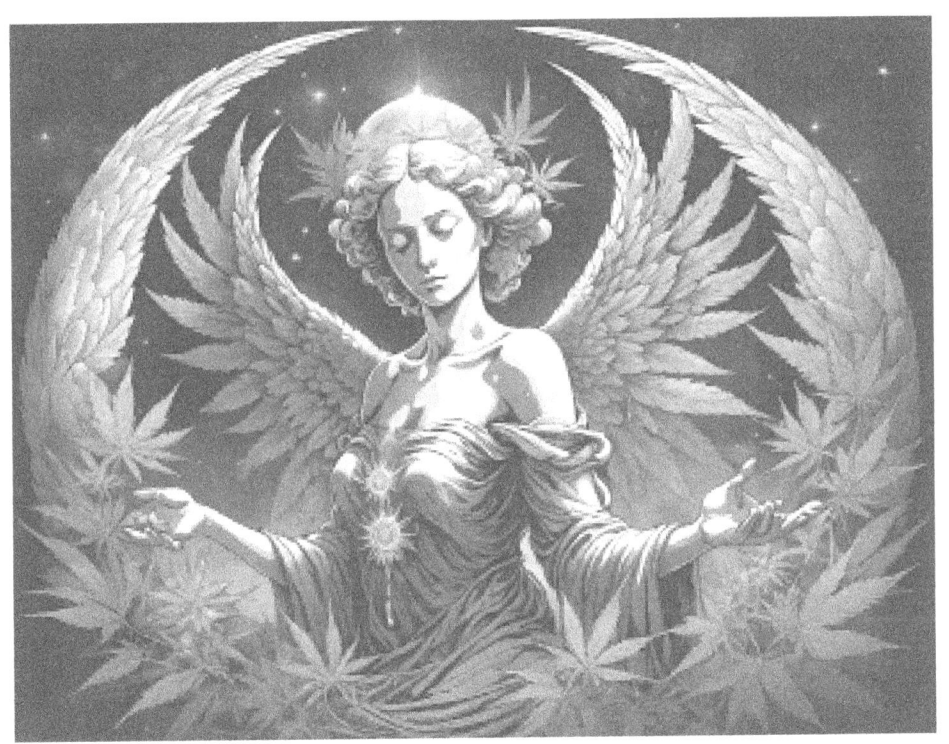

JedidiahDrotar

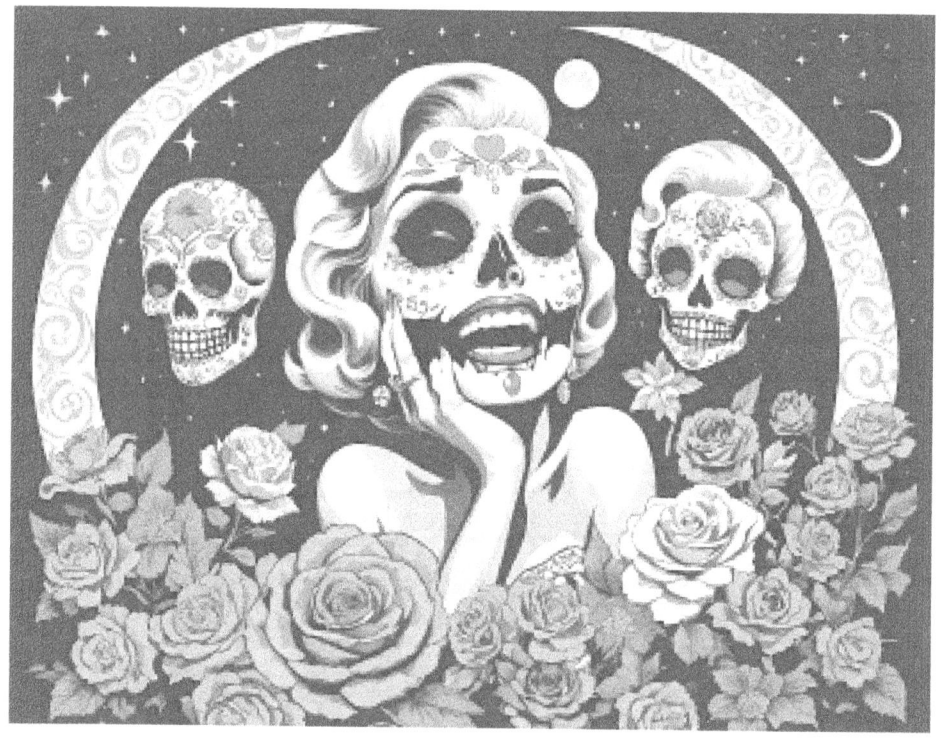

Tripping Hard or Hardly Tripping

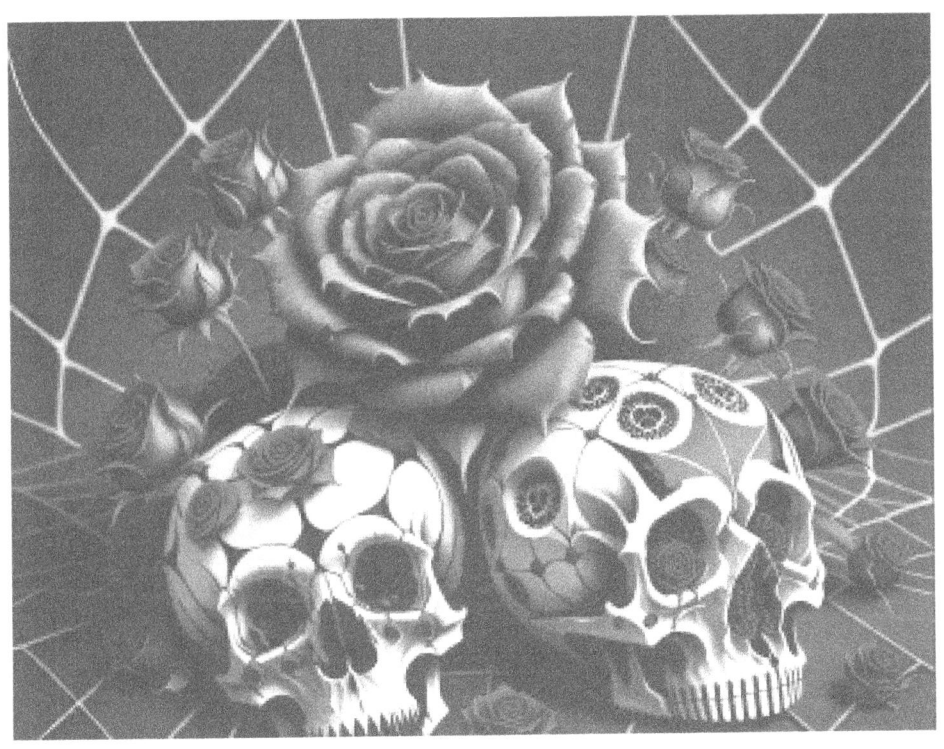

JedidiahDrotar

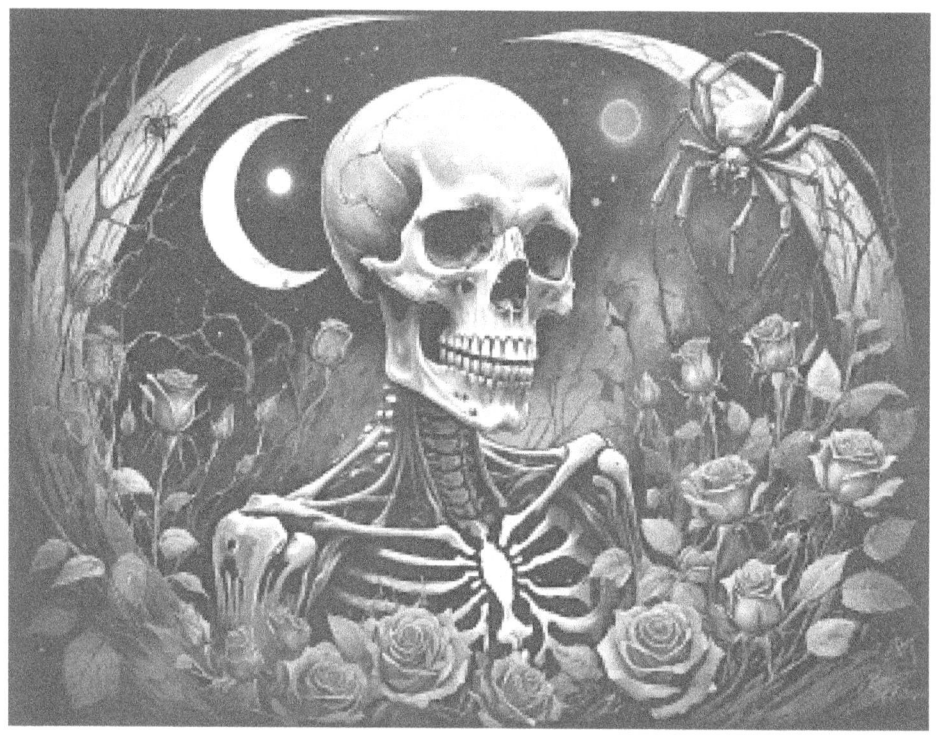

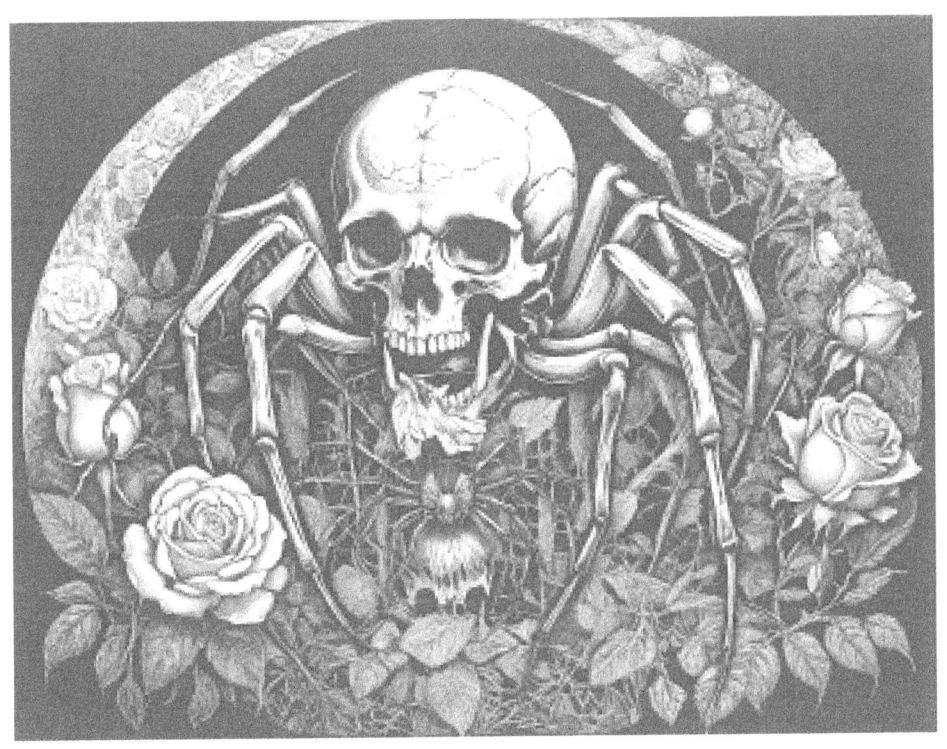

JedidiahDrotar

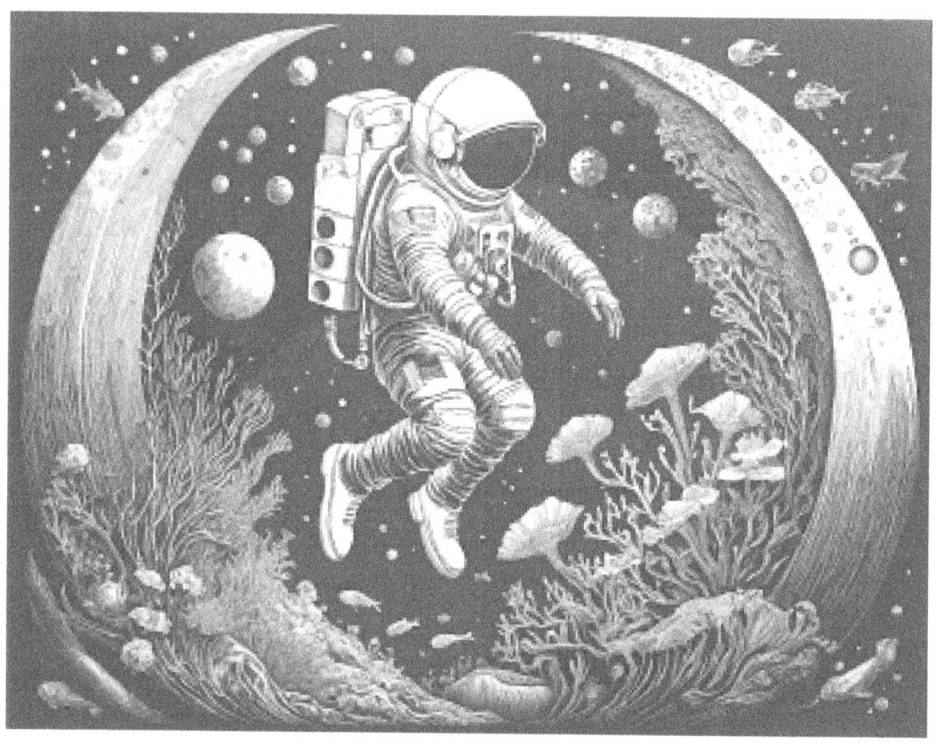

Tripping Hard or Hardly Tripping

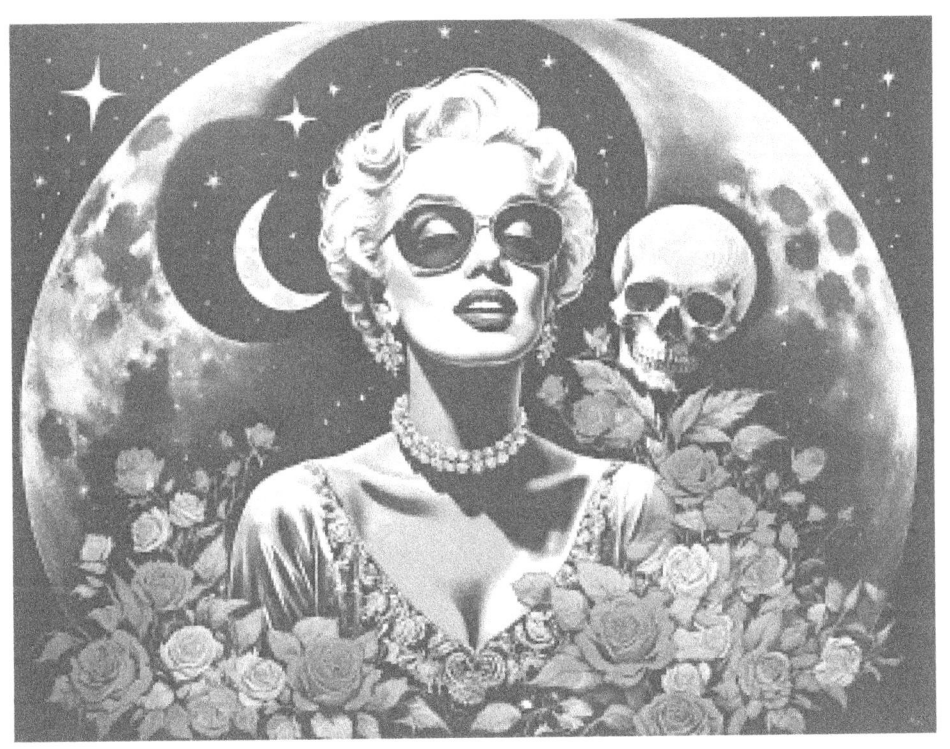

JedidiahDrotar

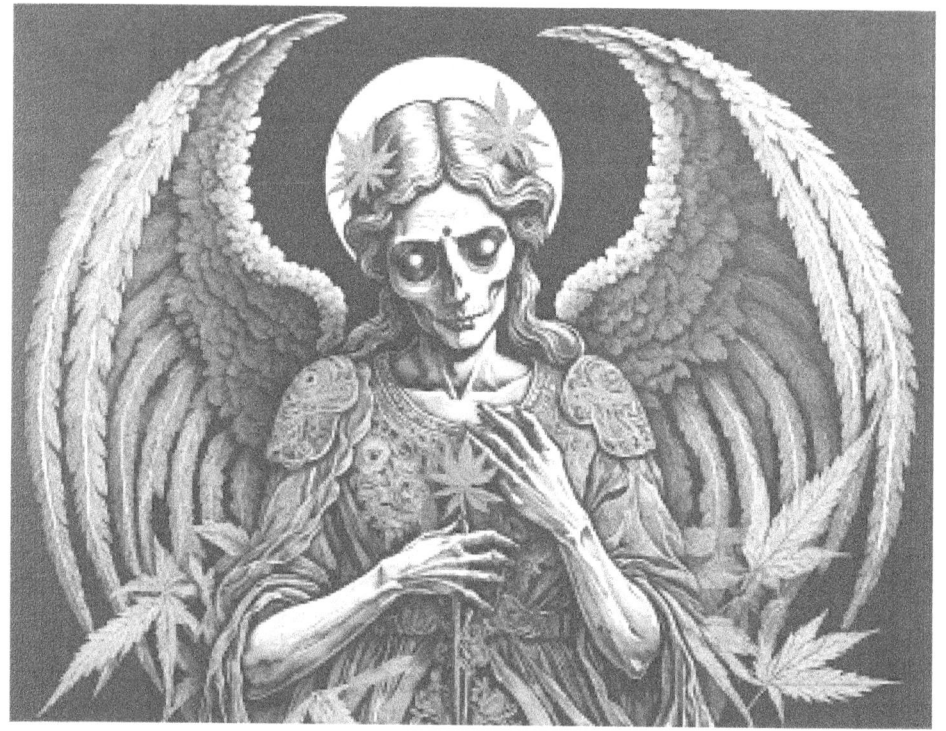

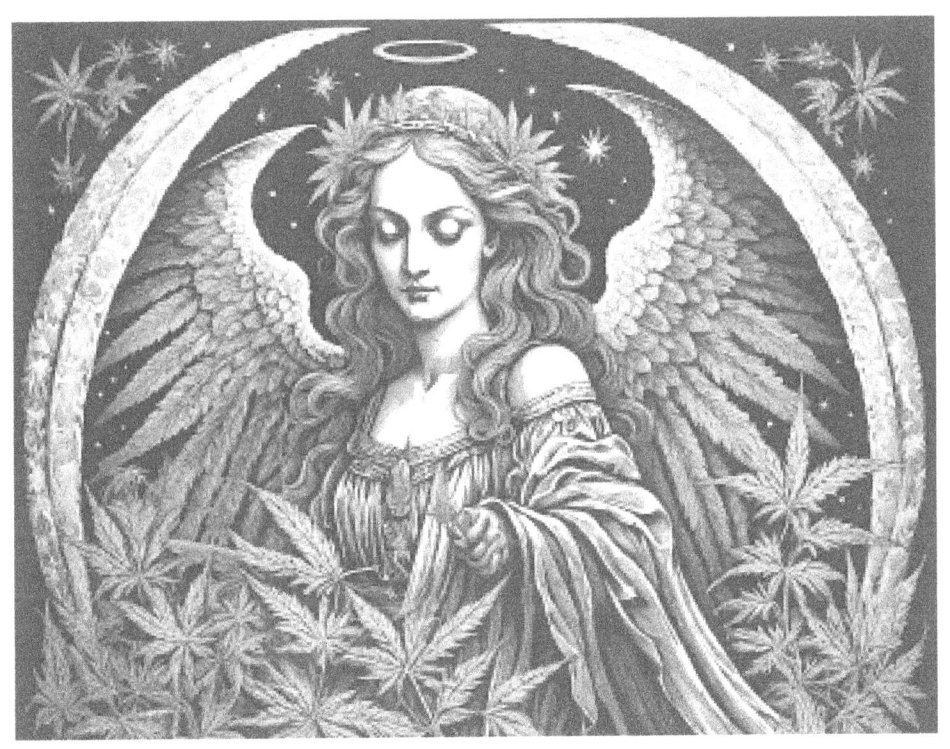

JedidiahDrotar

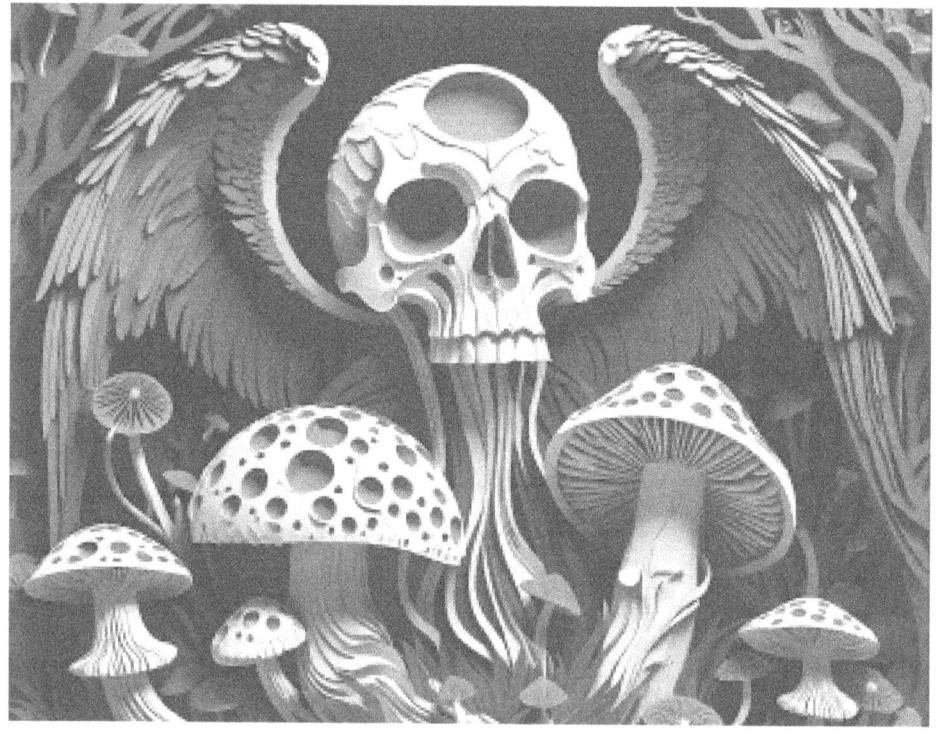

Tripping Hard or Hardly Tripping

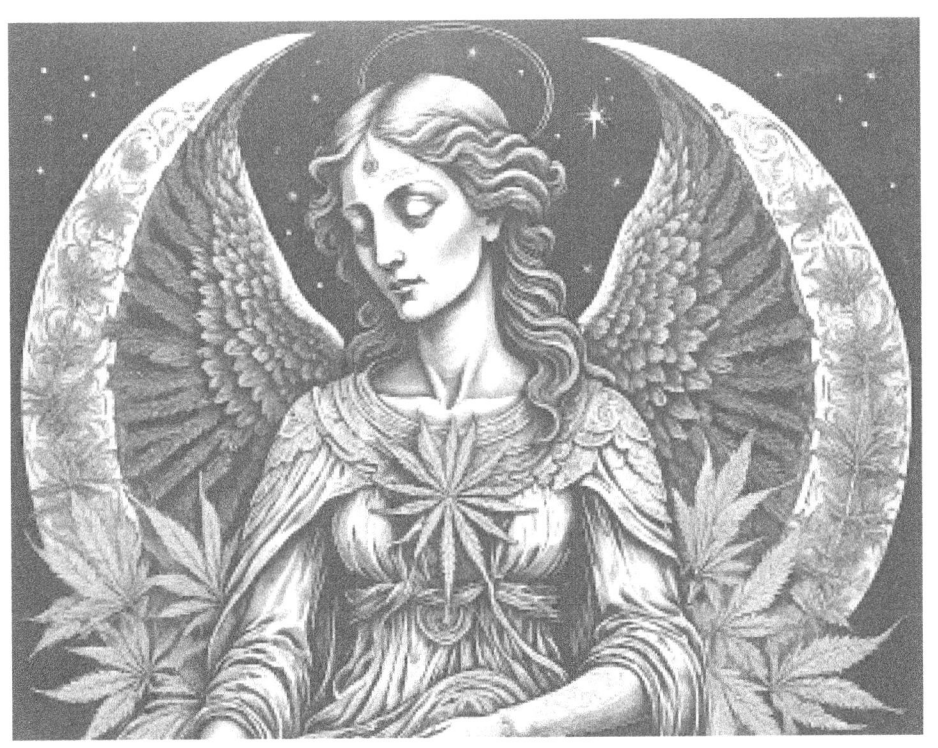

JedidiahDrotar

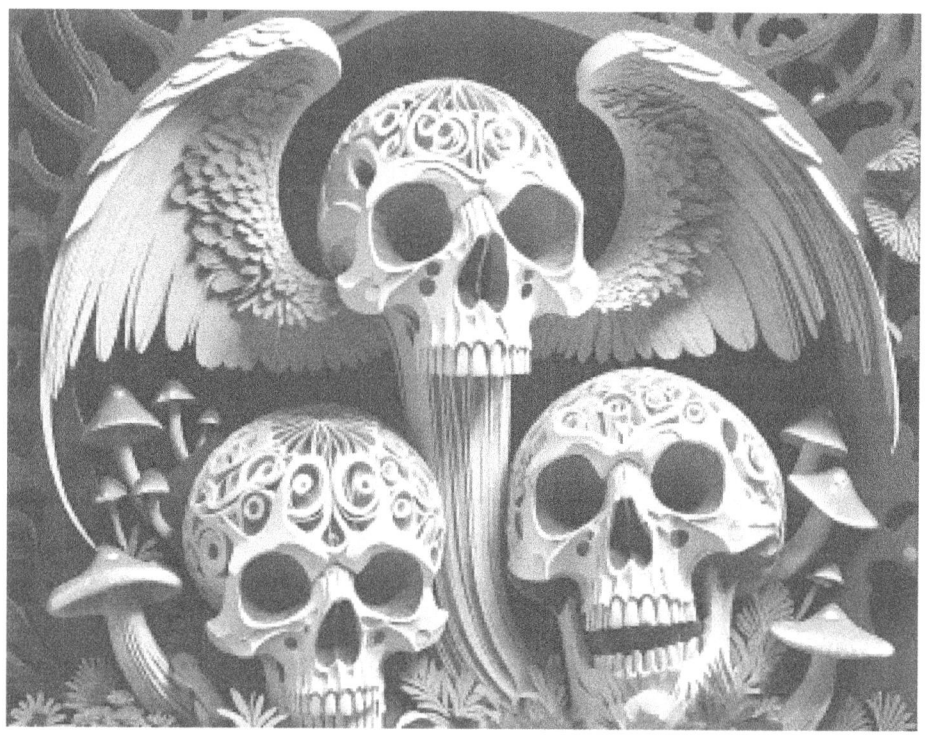

Tripping Hard or Hardly Tripping

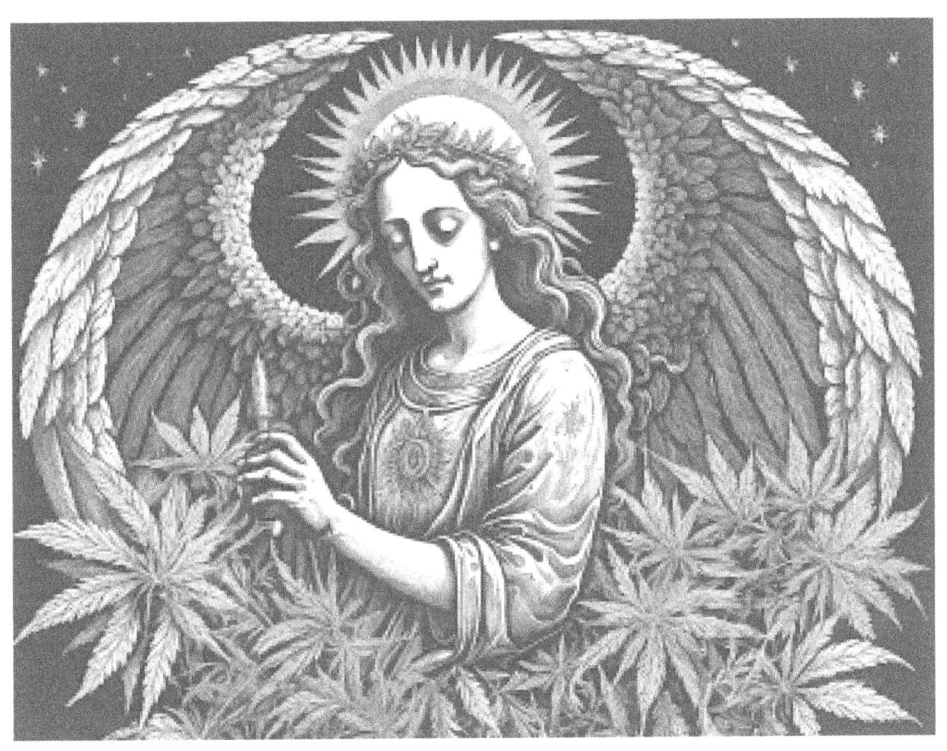

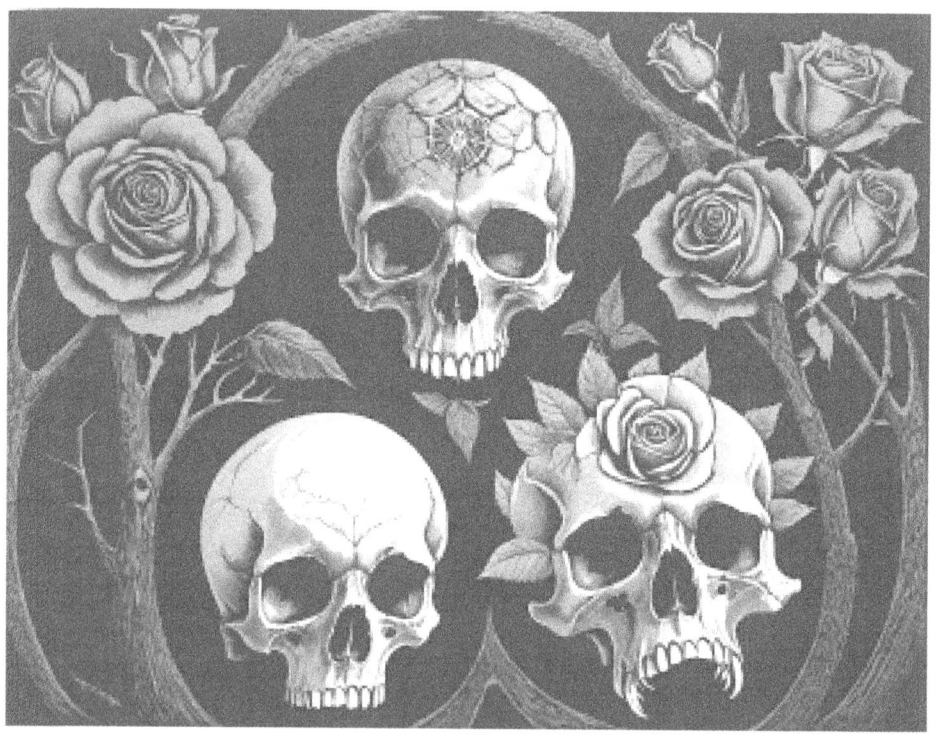

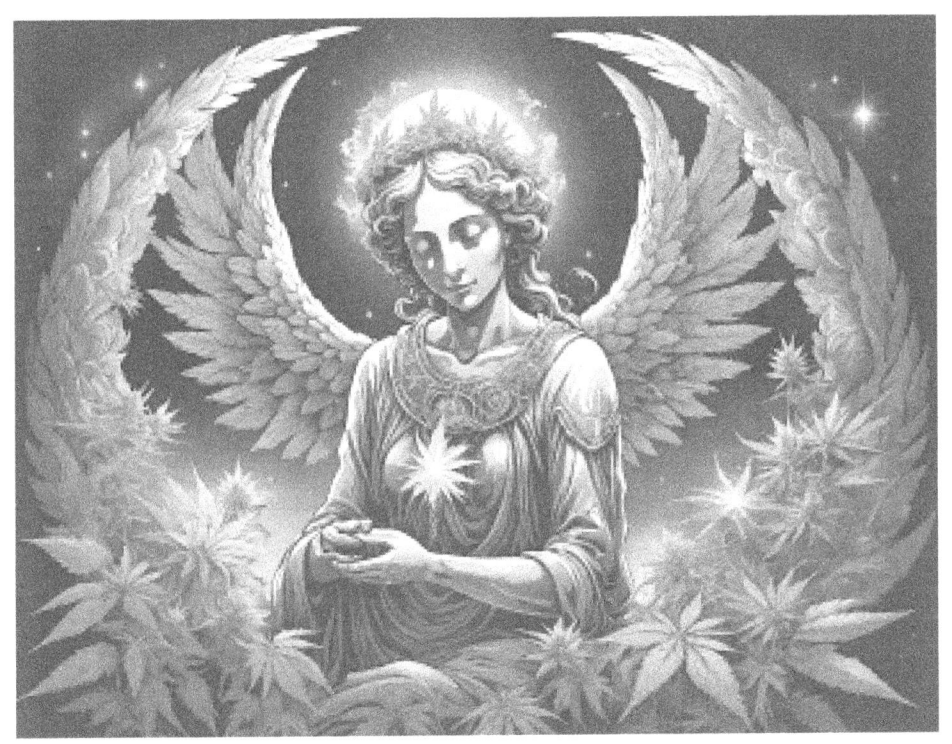

JedidiahDrotar

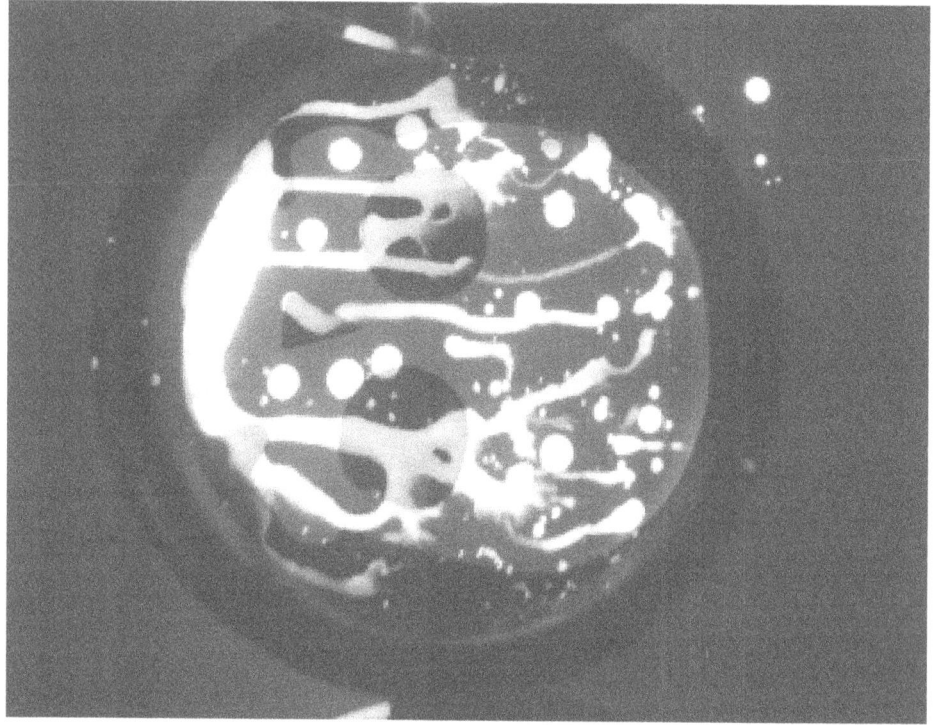

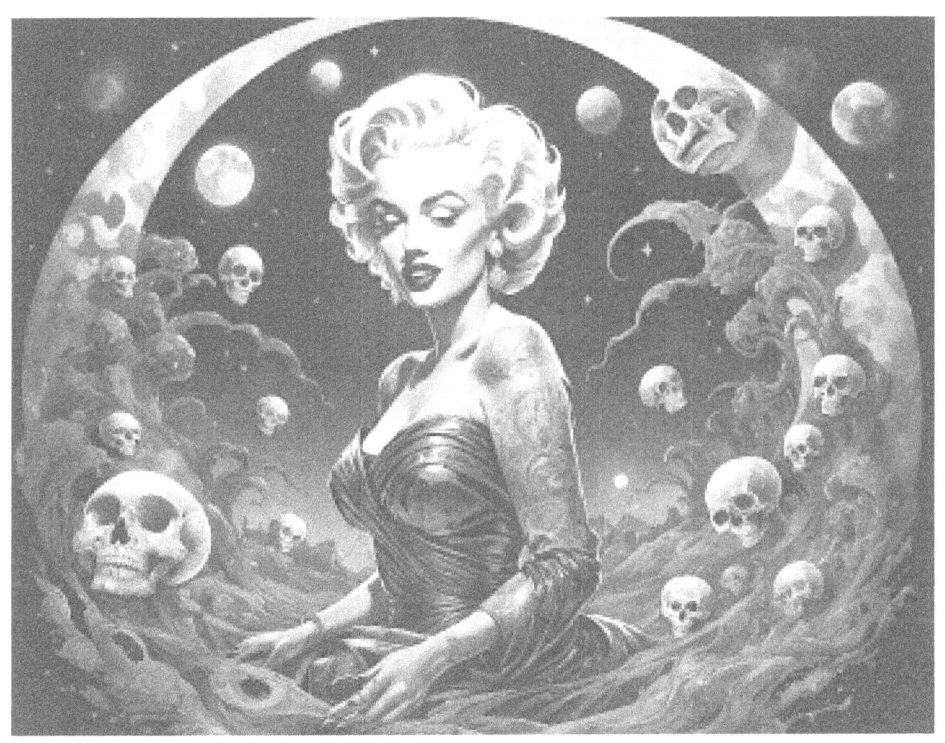

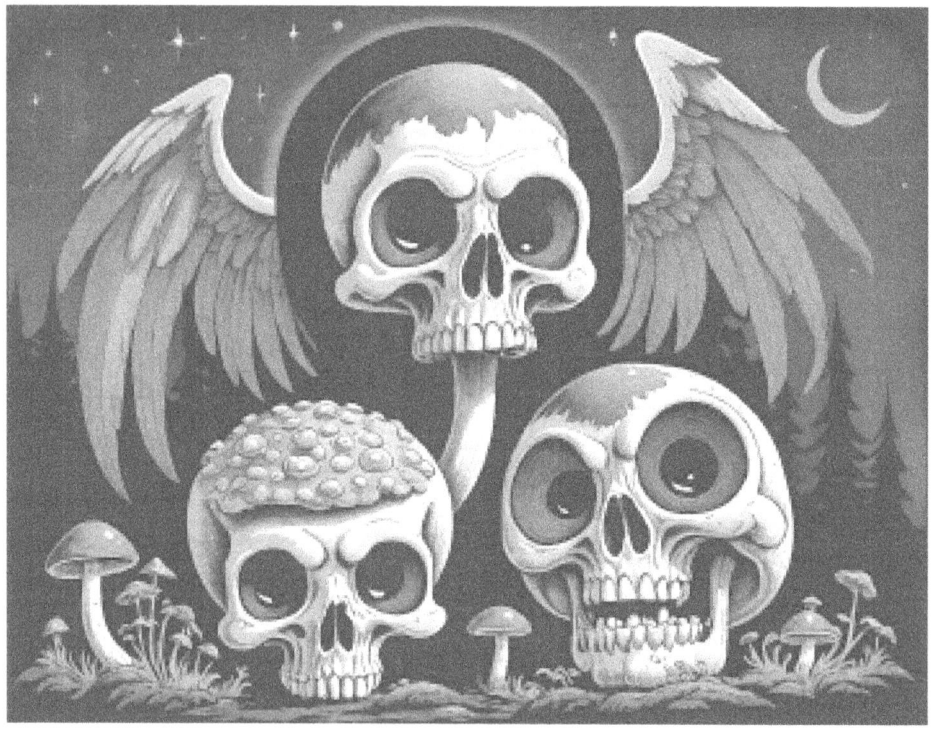

Tripping Hard or Hardly Tripping

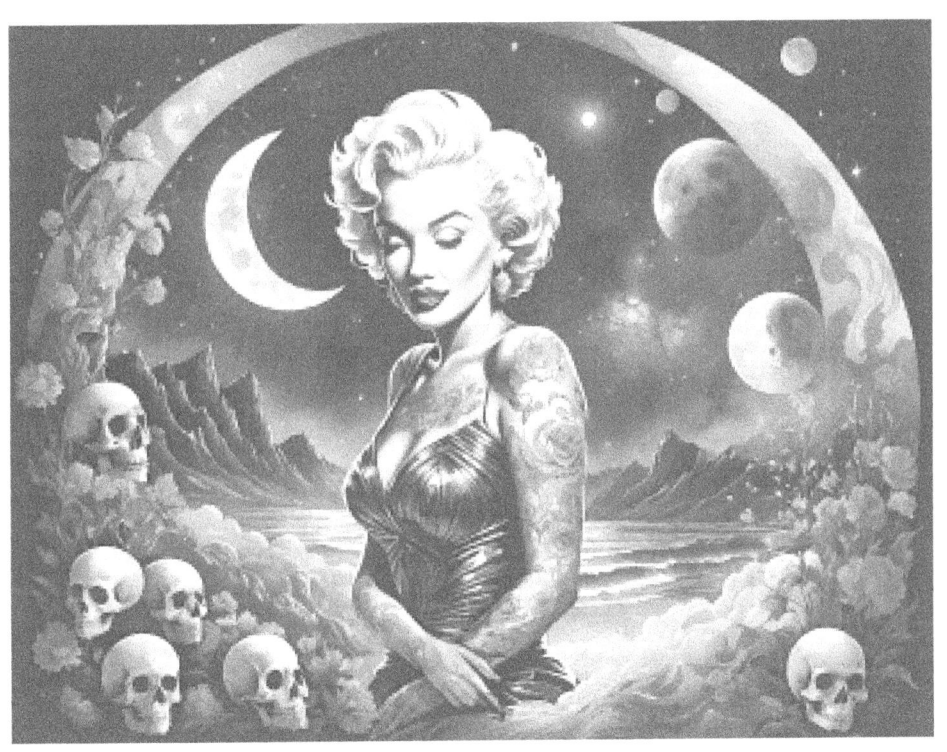

JedidiahDrotar

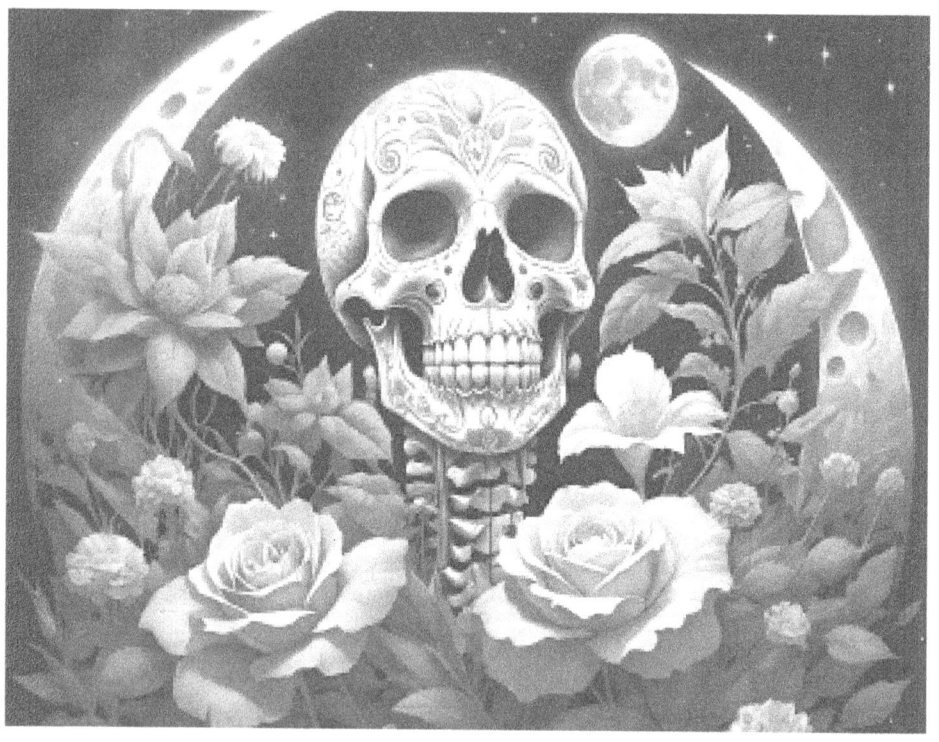

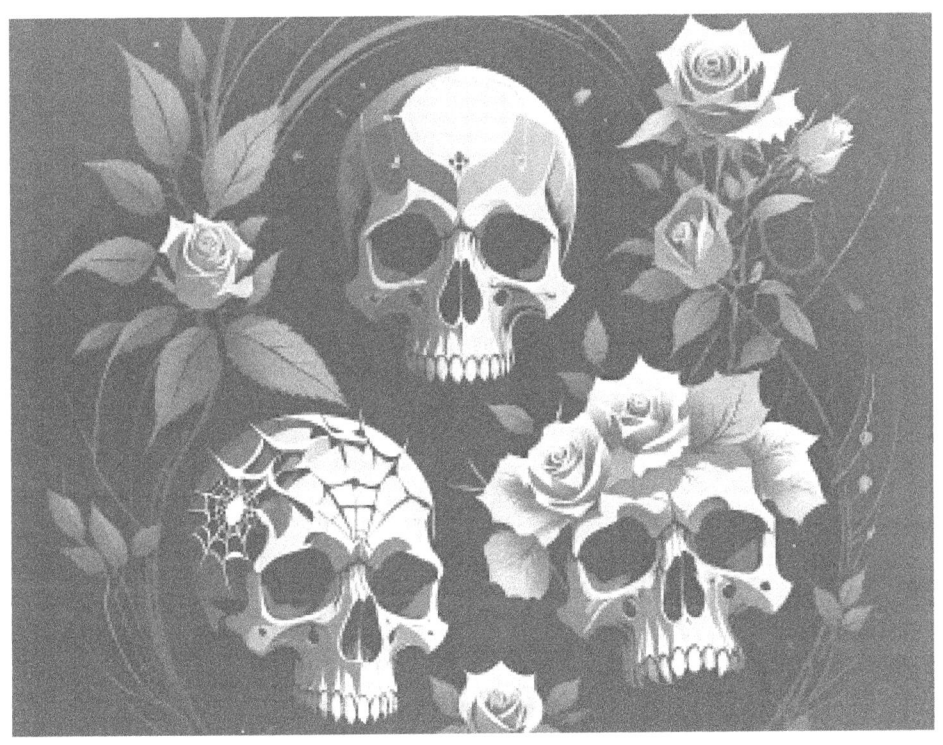

JedidiahDrotar

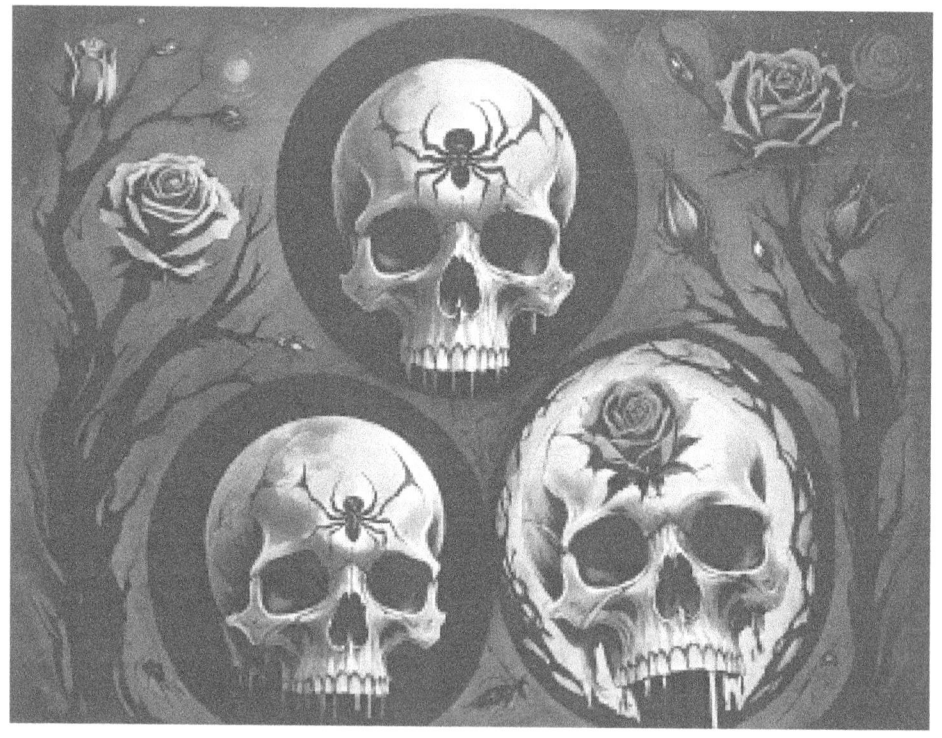

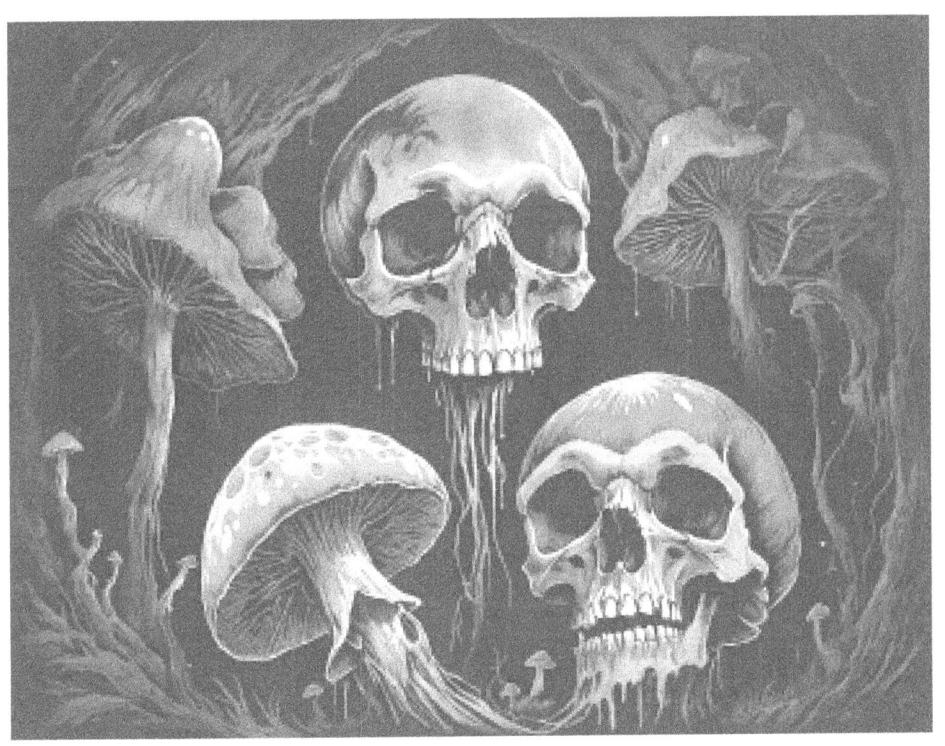

JedidiahDrotar

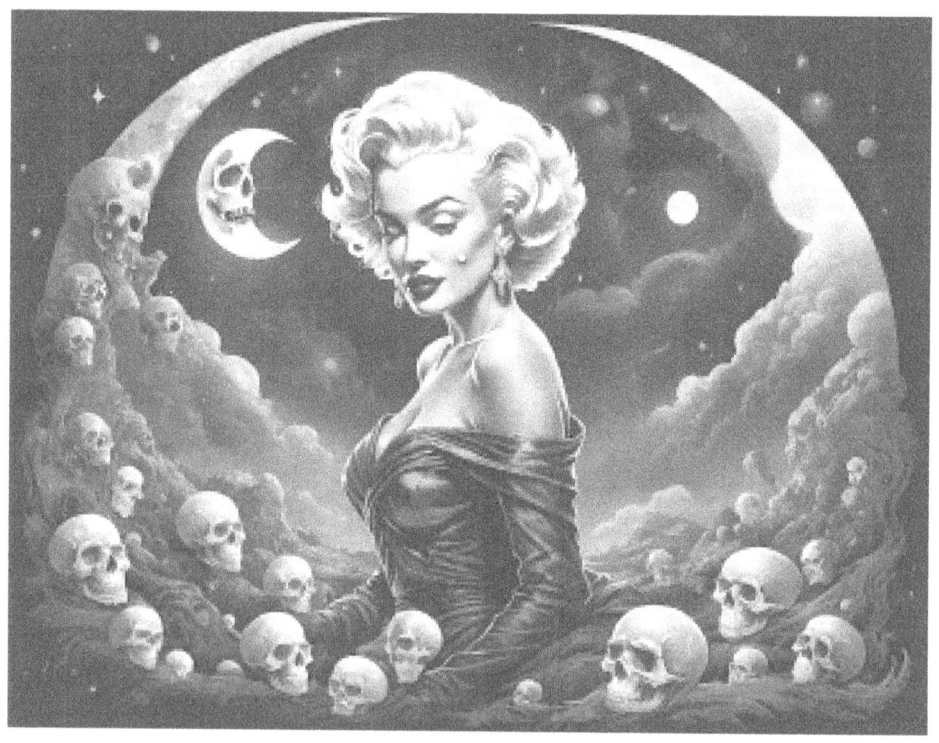

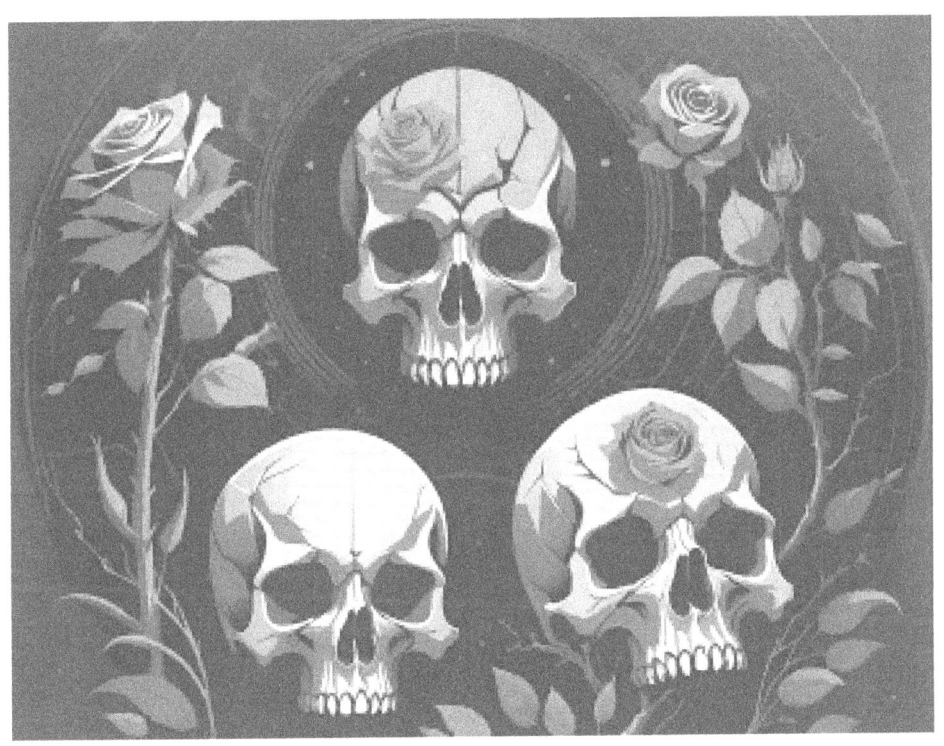

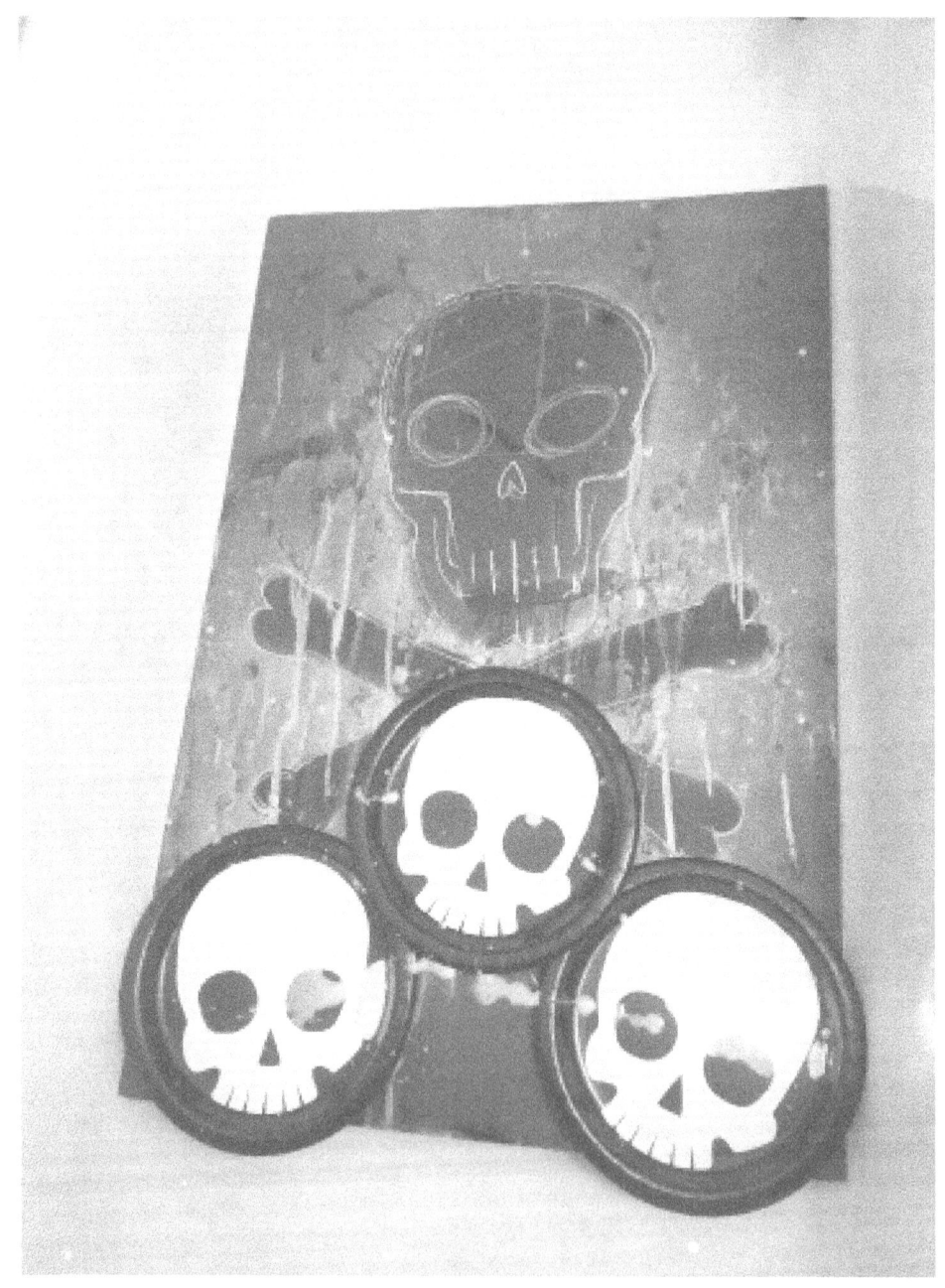

Tripping Hard or Hardly Tripping

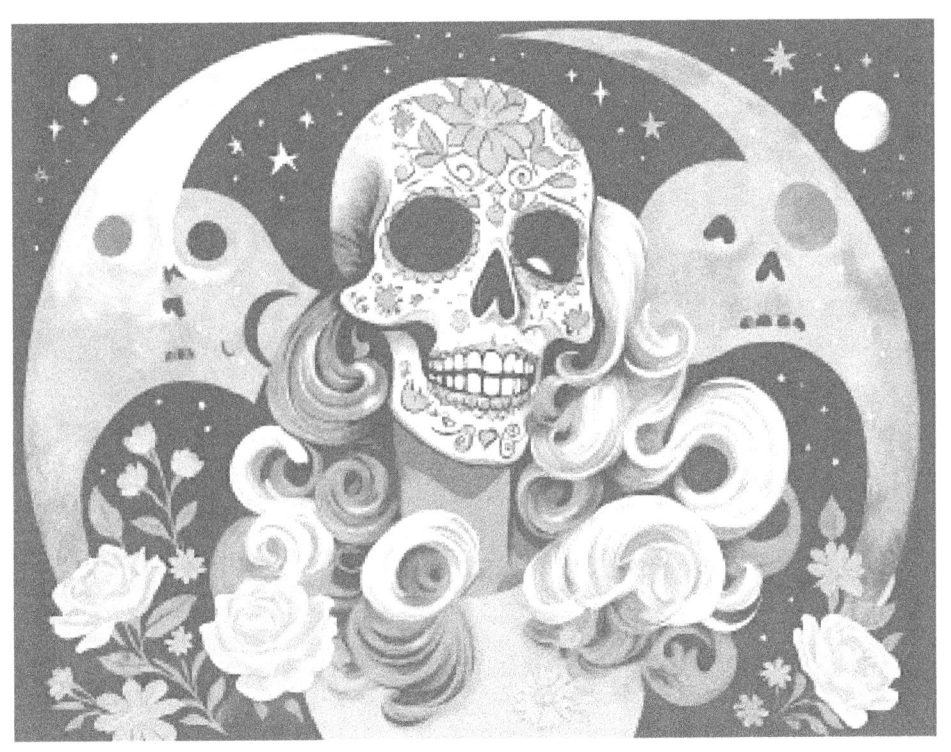

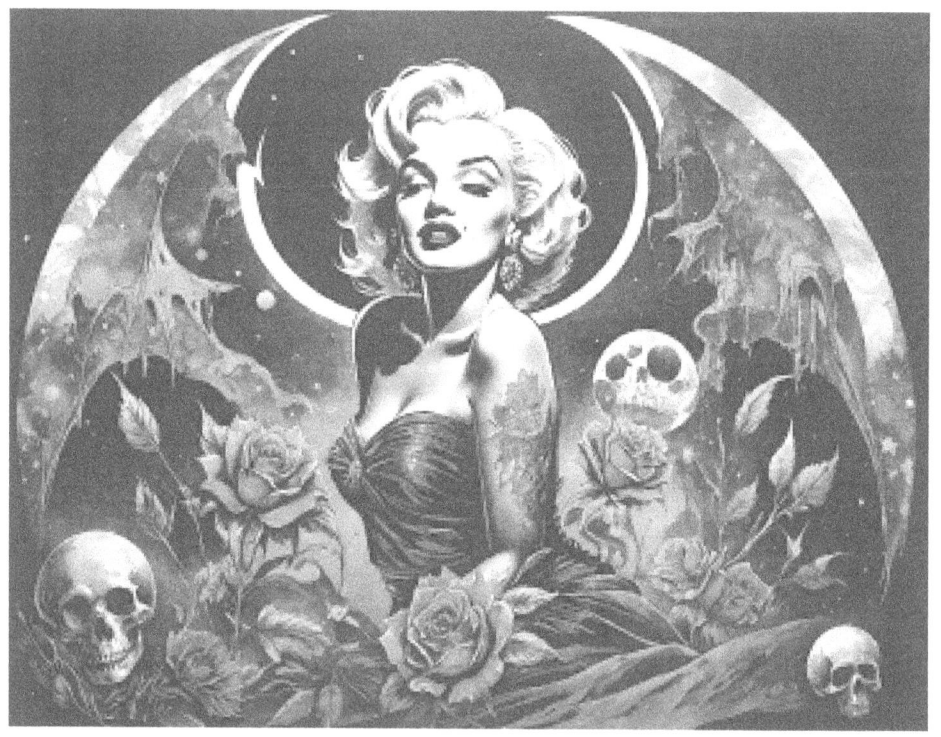

Tripping Hard or Hardly Tripping

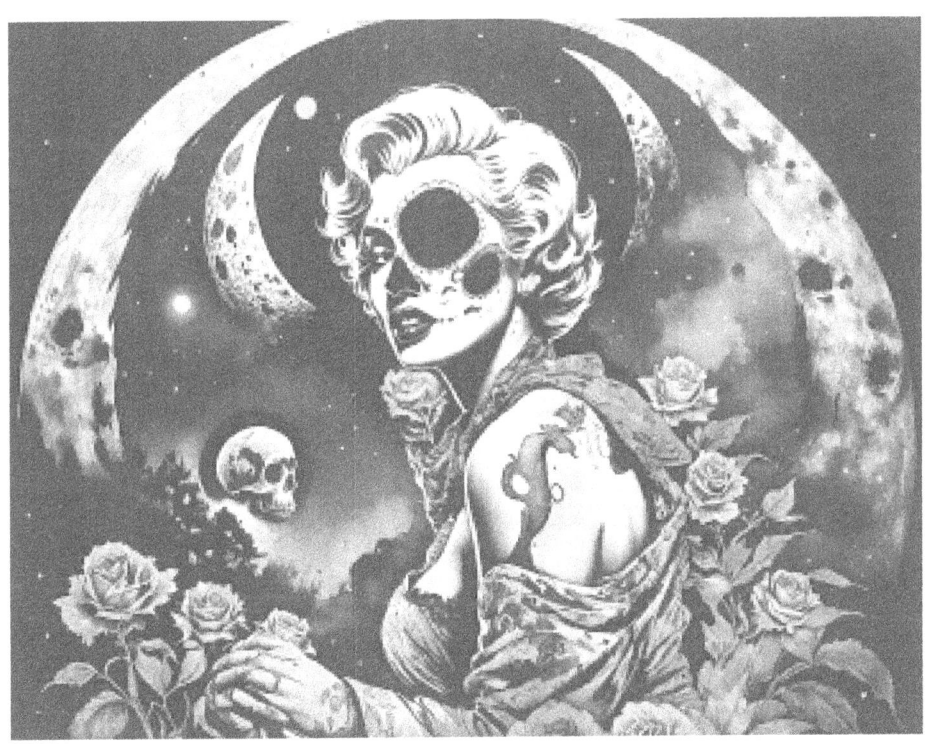

JedidiahDrotar

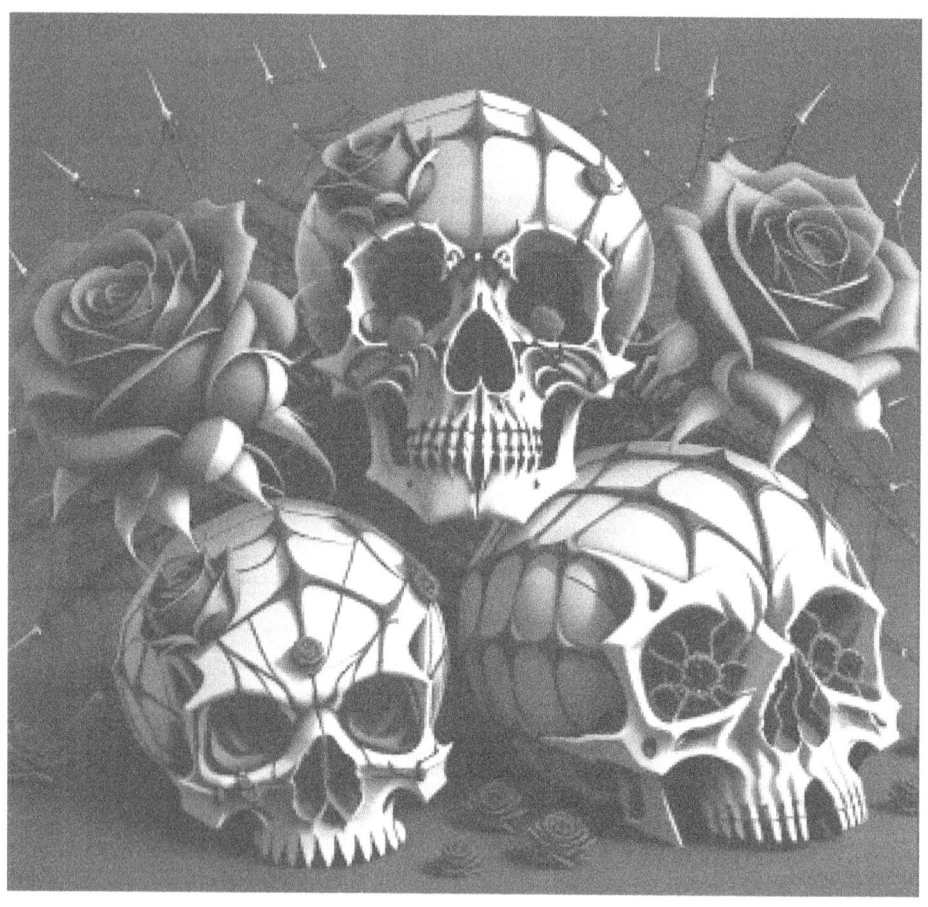

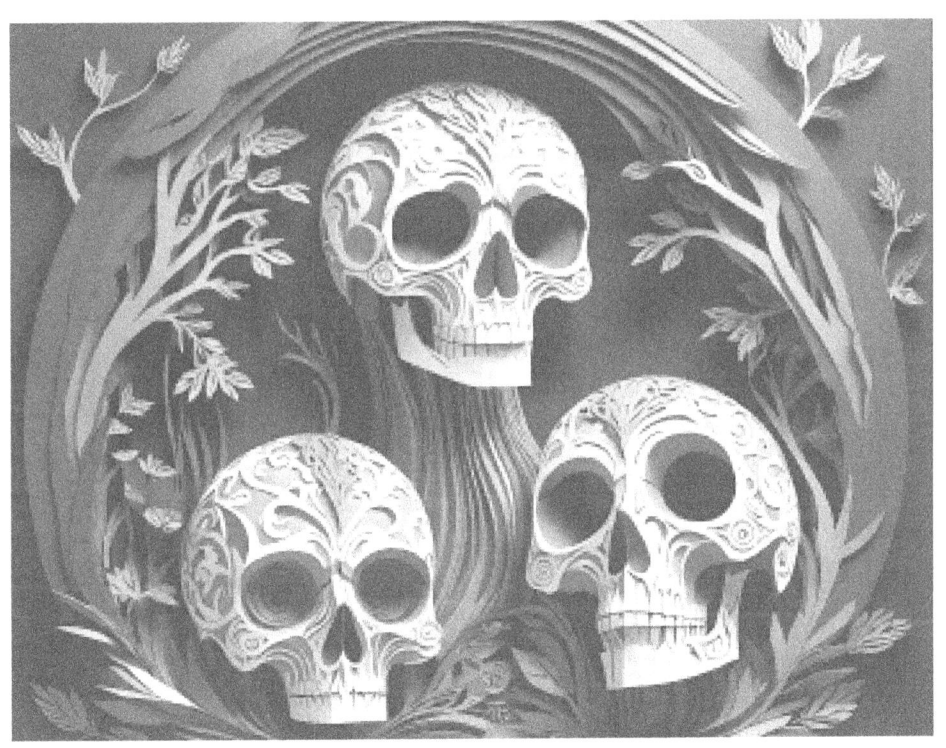

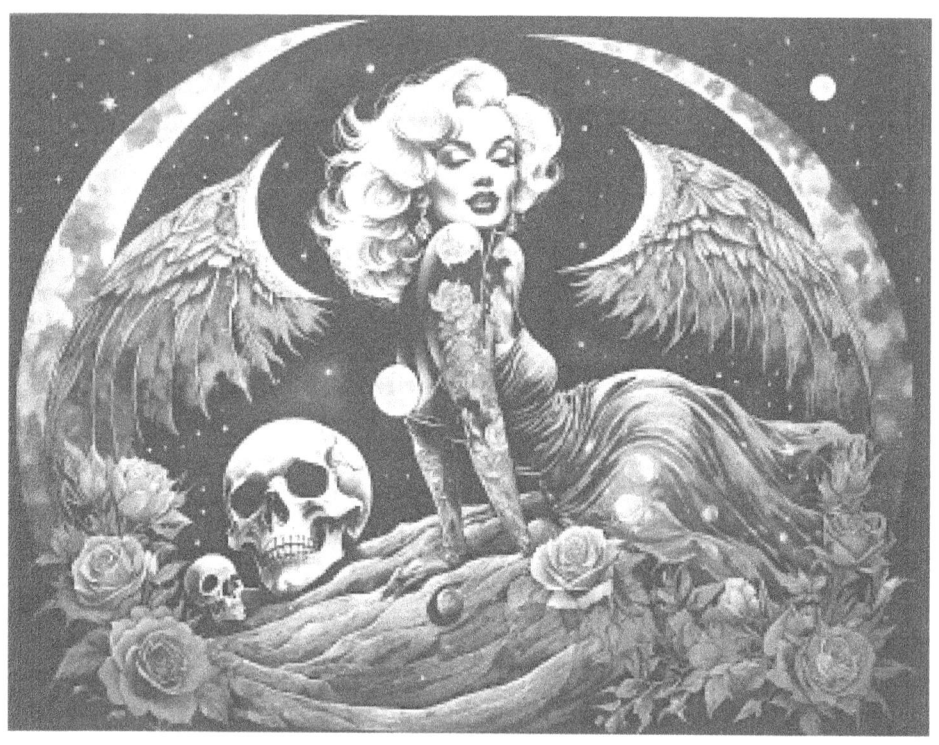

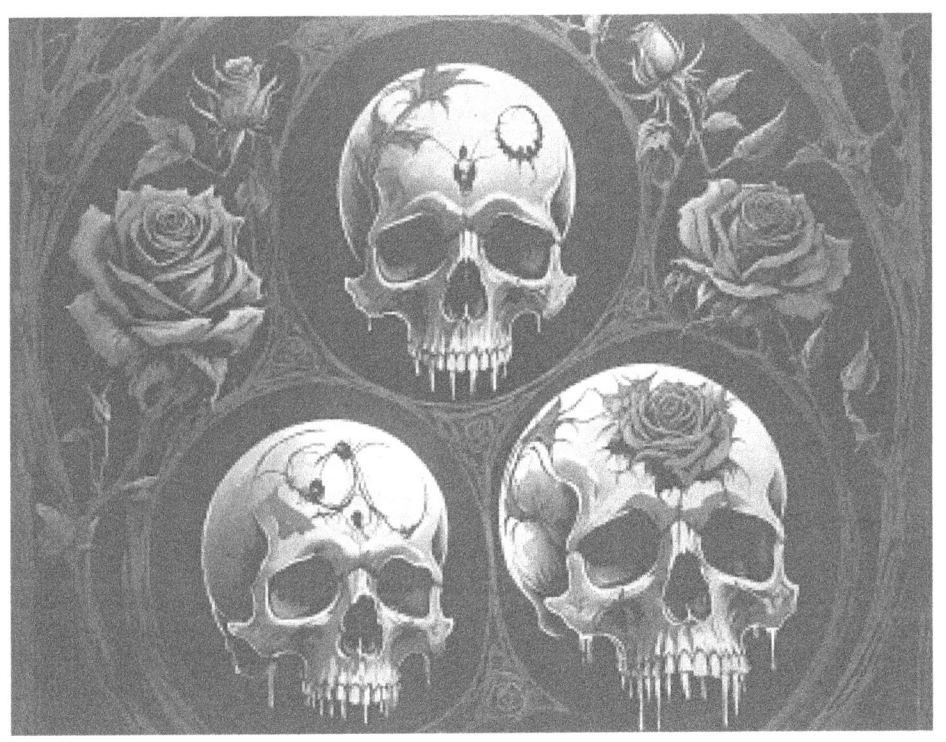

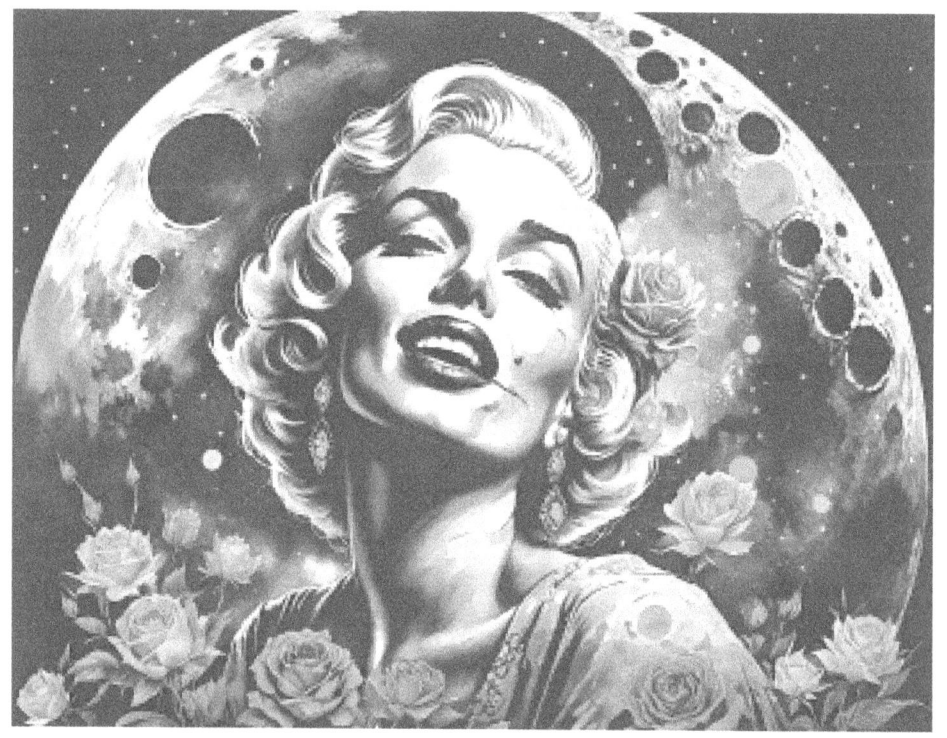

Tripping Hard or Hardly Tripping

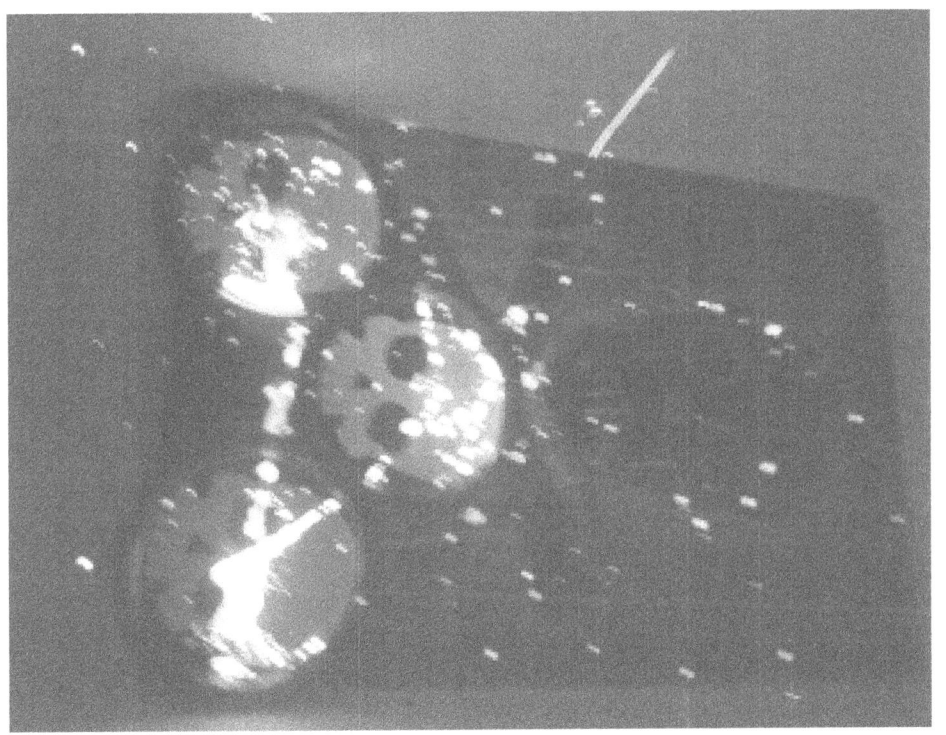

JedidiahDrotar

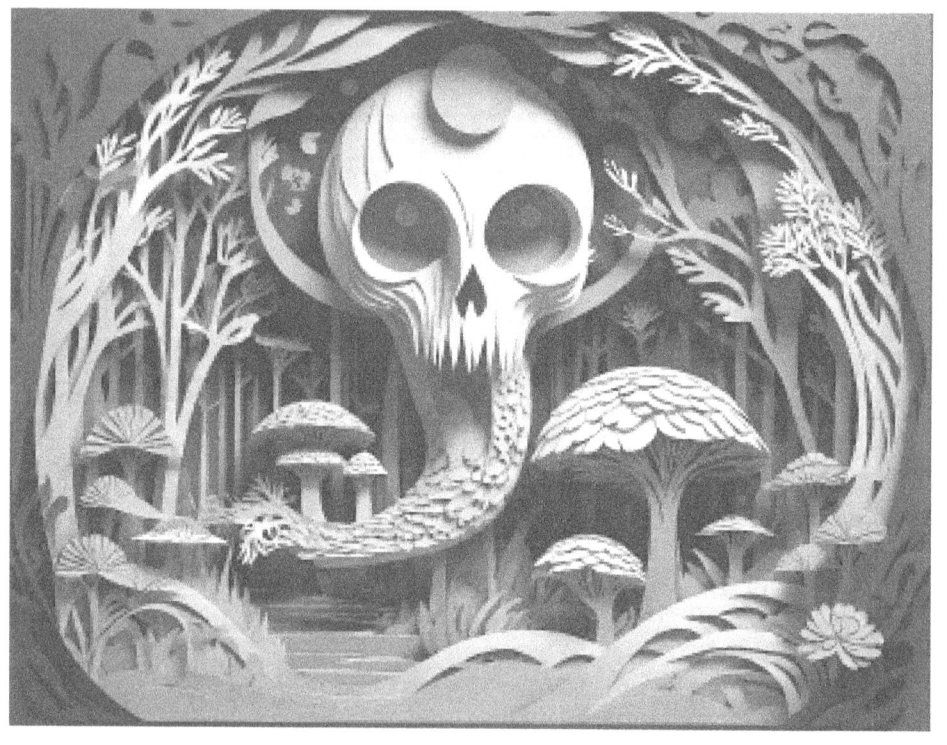

JedidiahDrotar

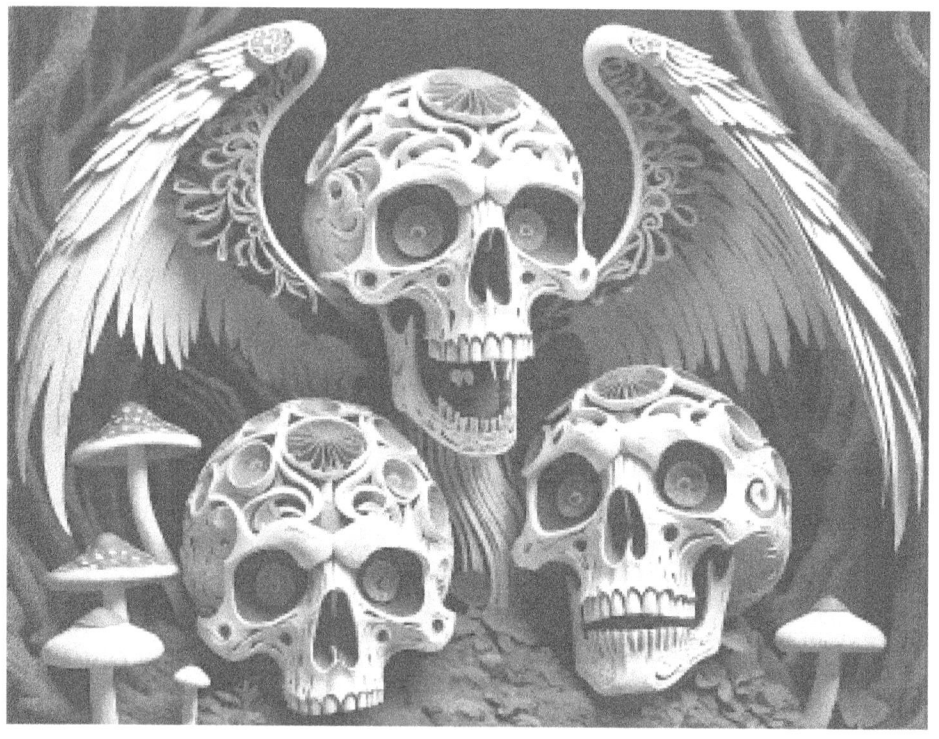

Tripping Hard or Hardly Tripping

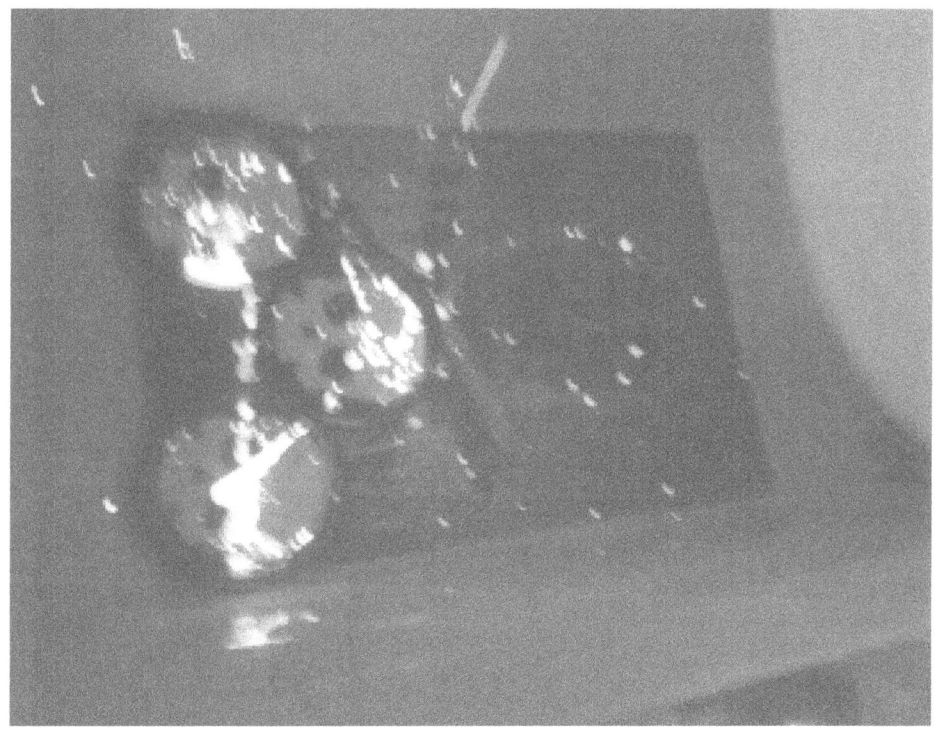

JedidiahDrotar

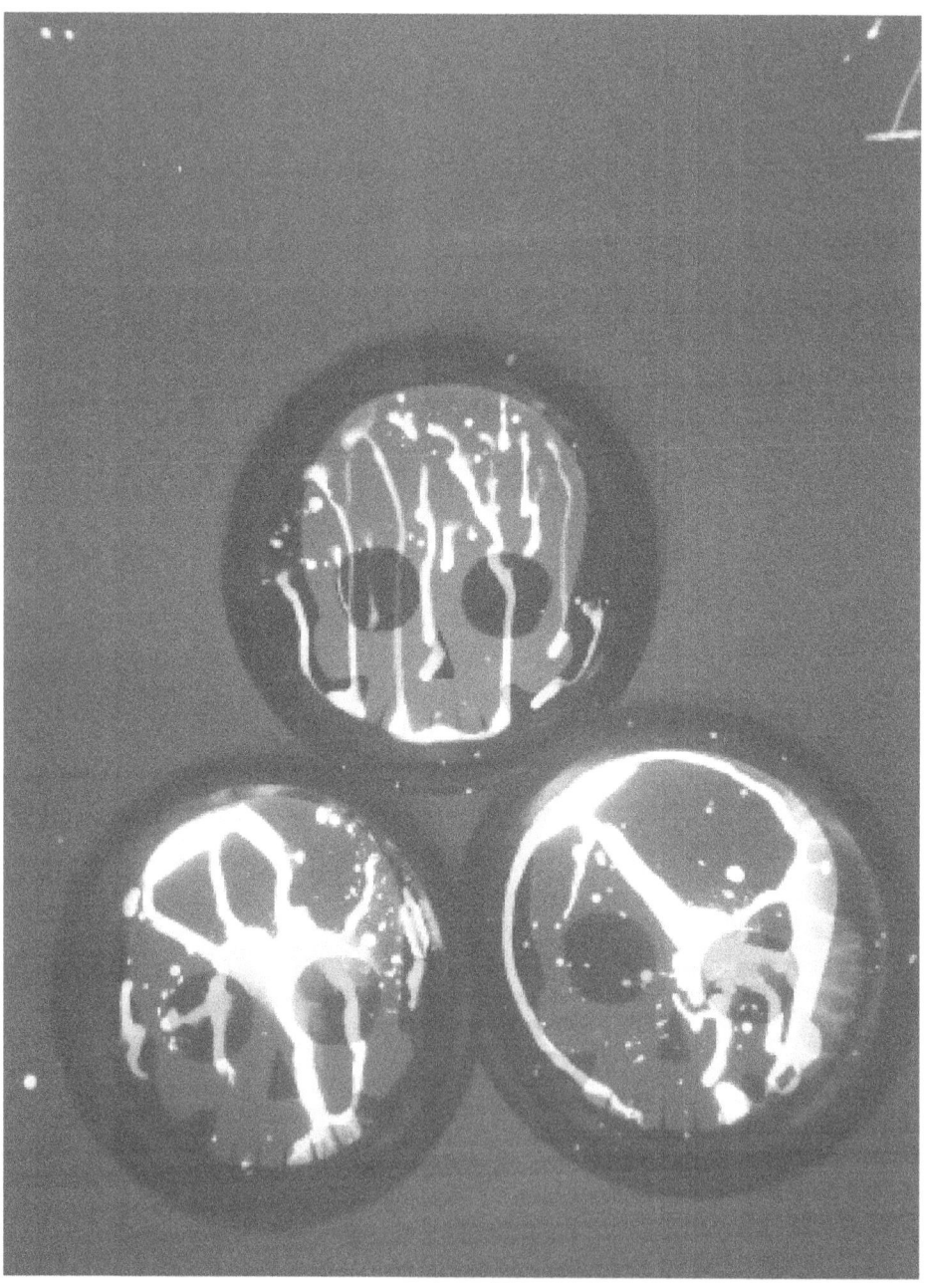

Tripping Hard or Hardly Tripping

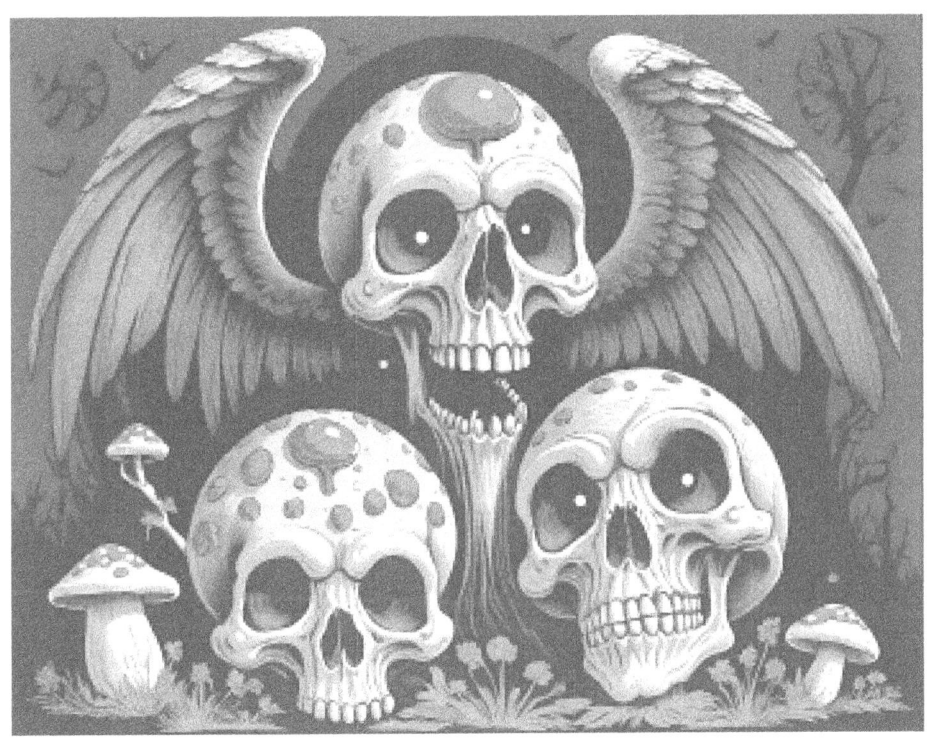

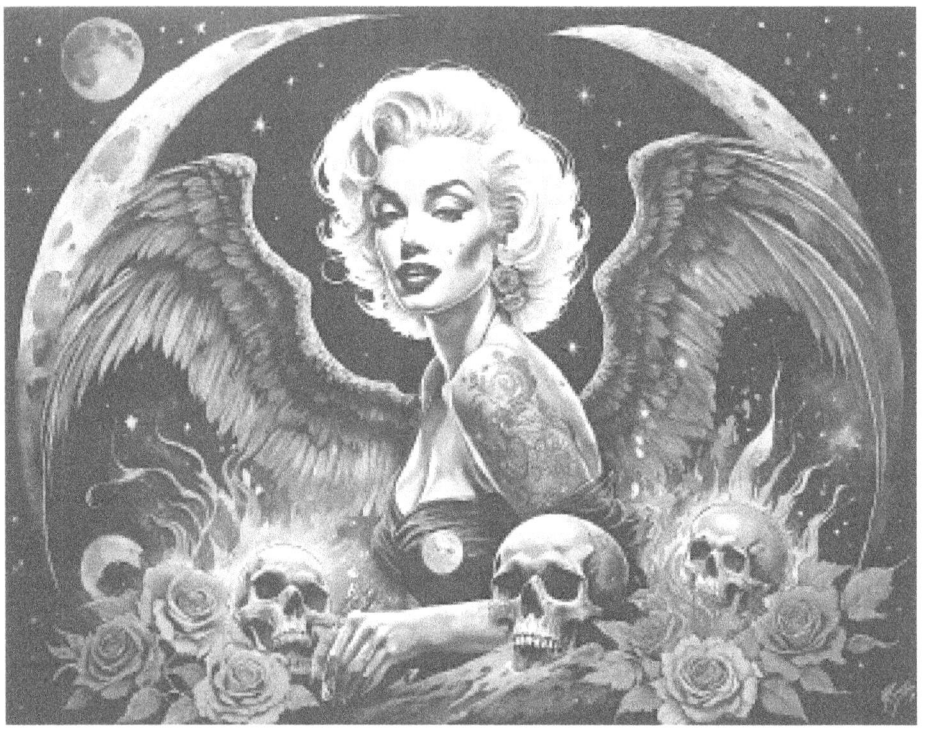

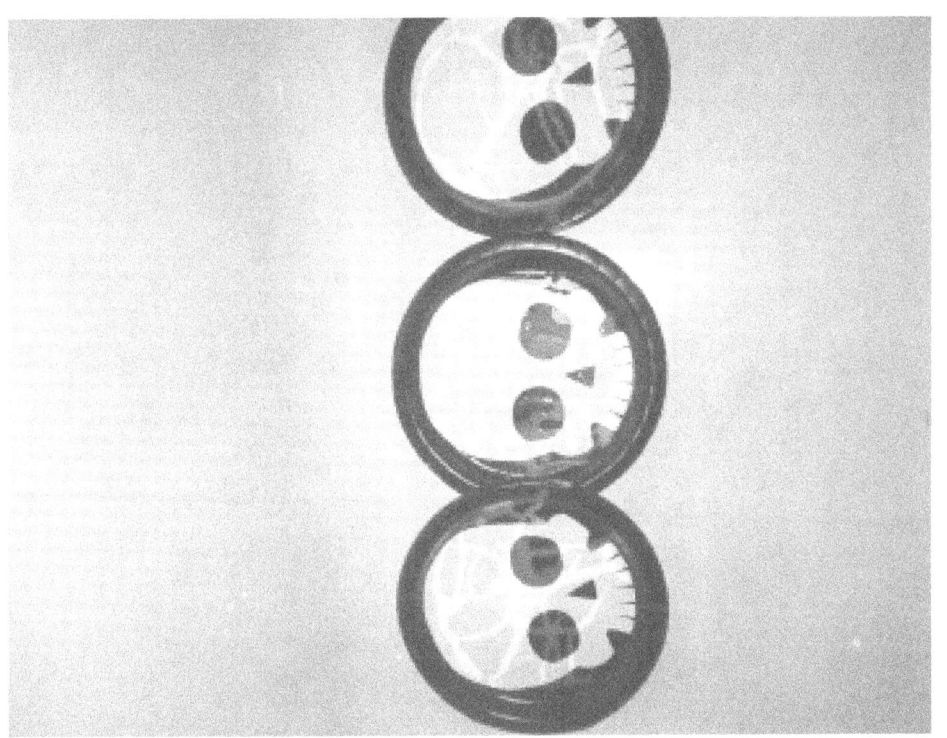

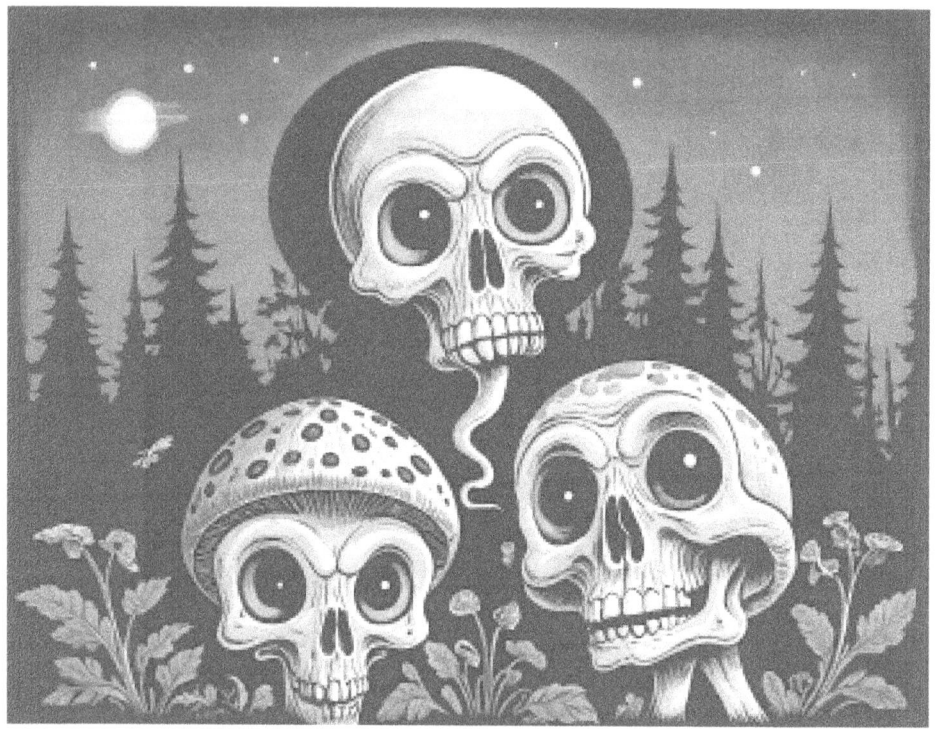

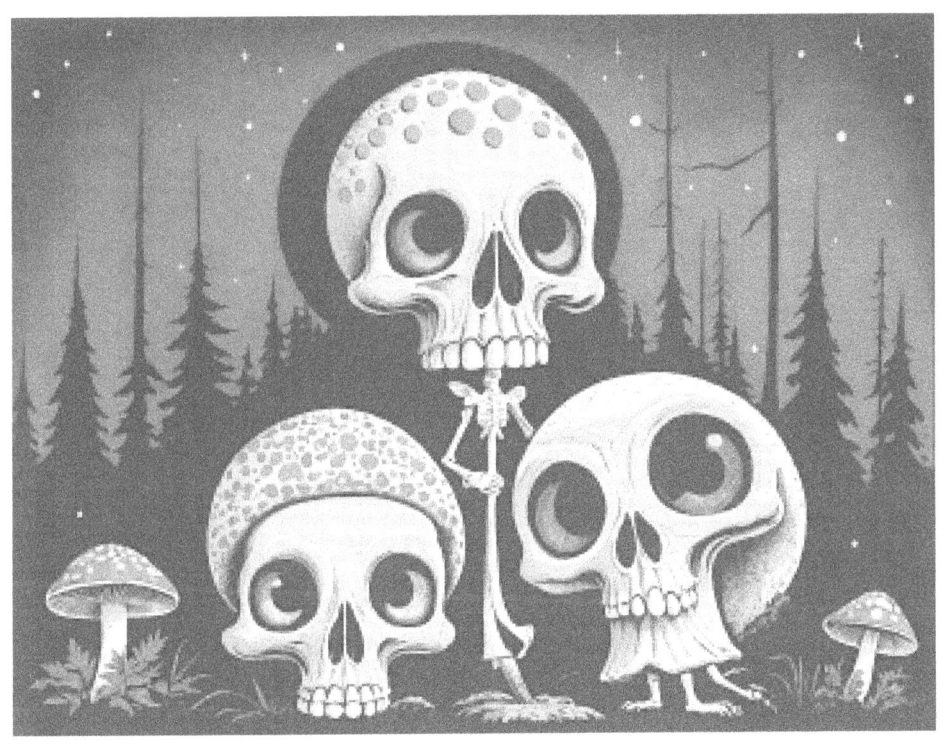

JedidiahDrotar

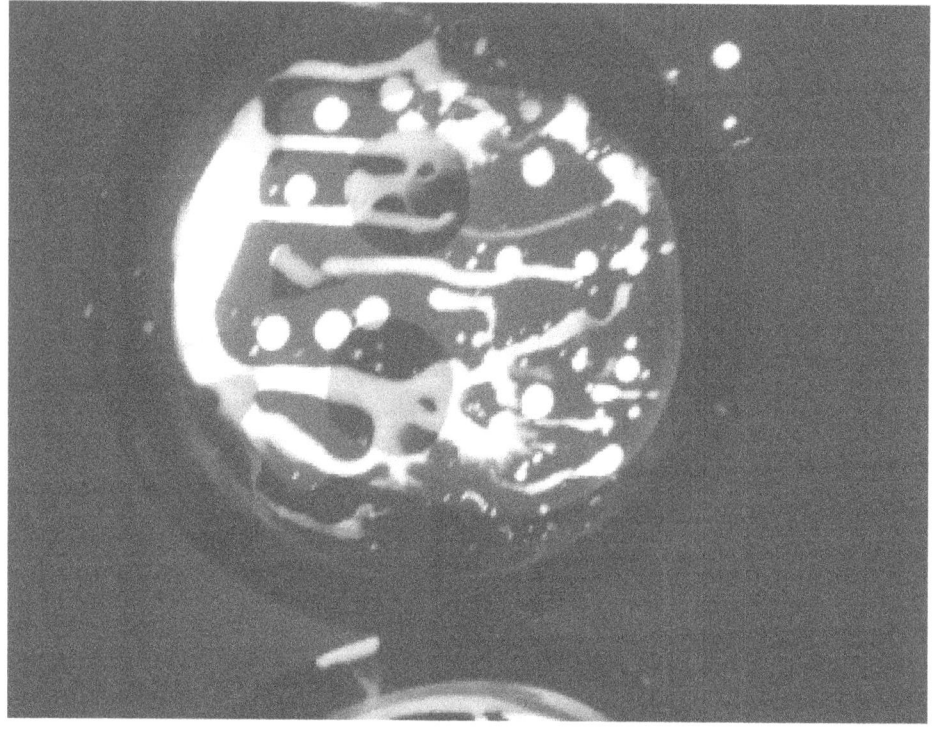

Tripping Hard or Hardly Tripping

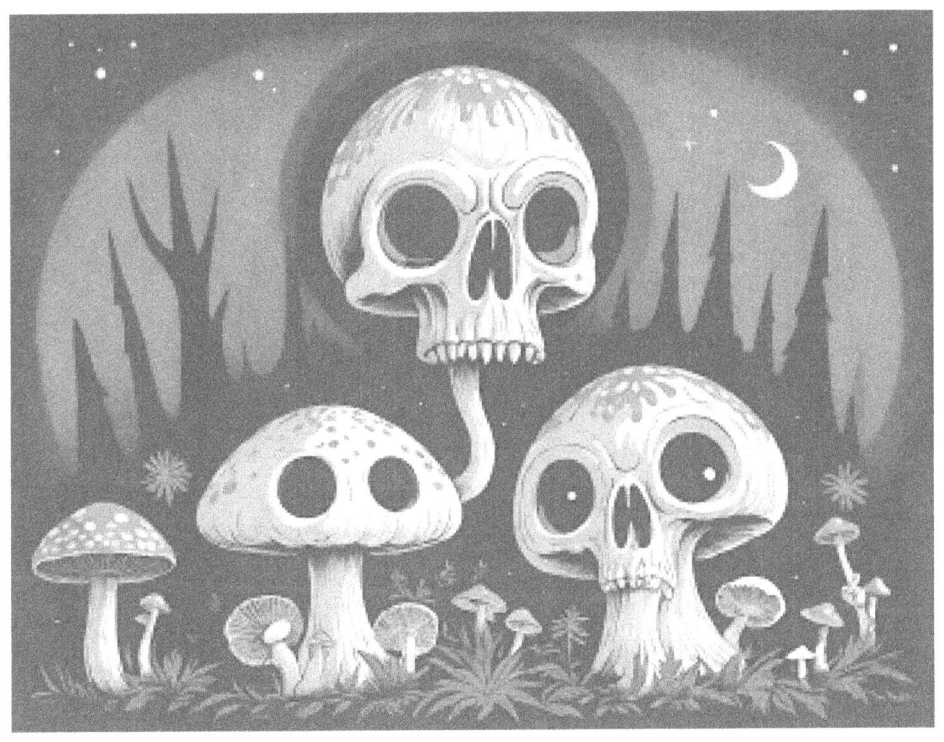

JedidiahDrotar

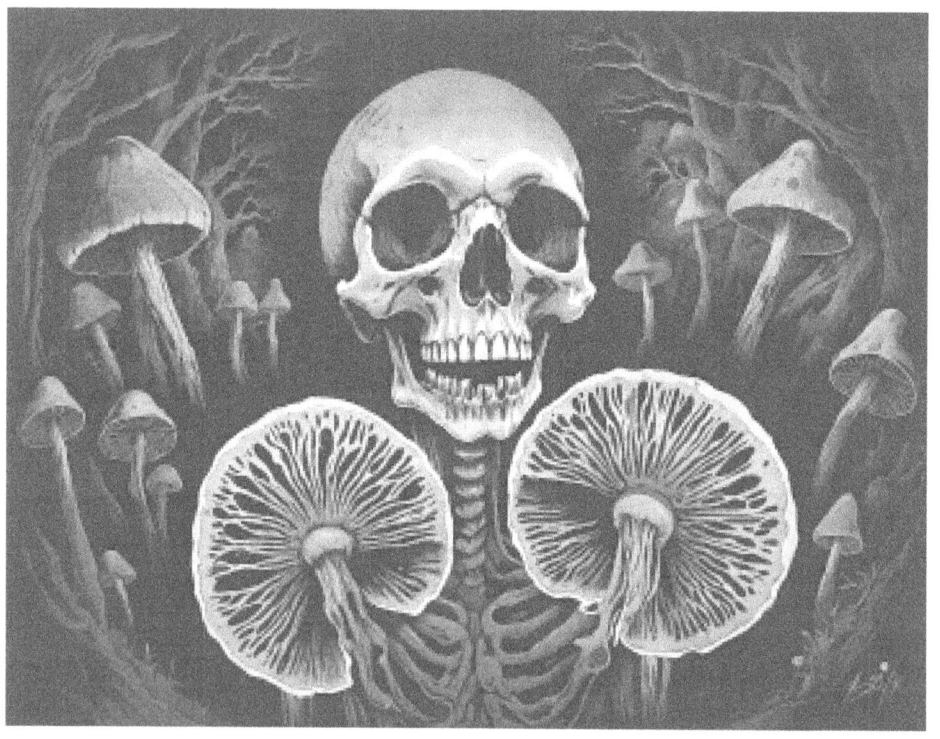

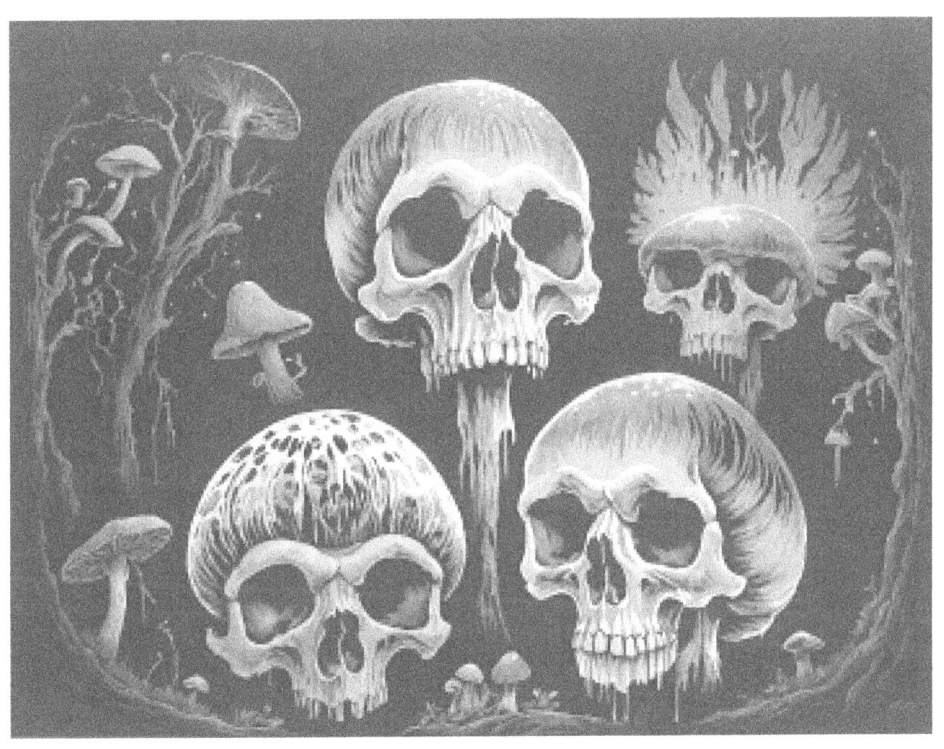

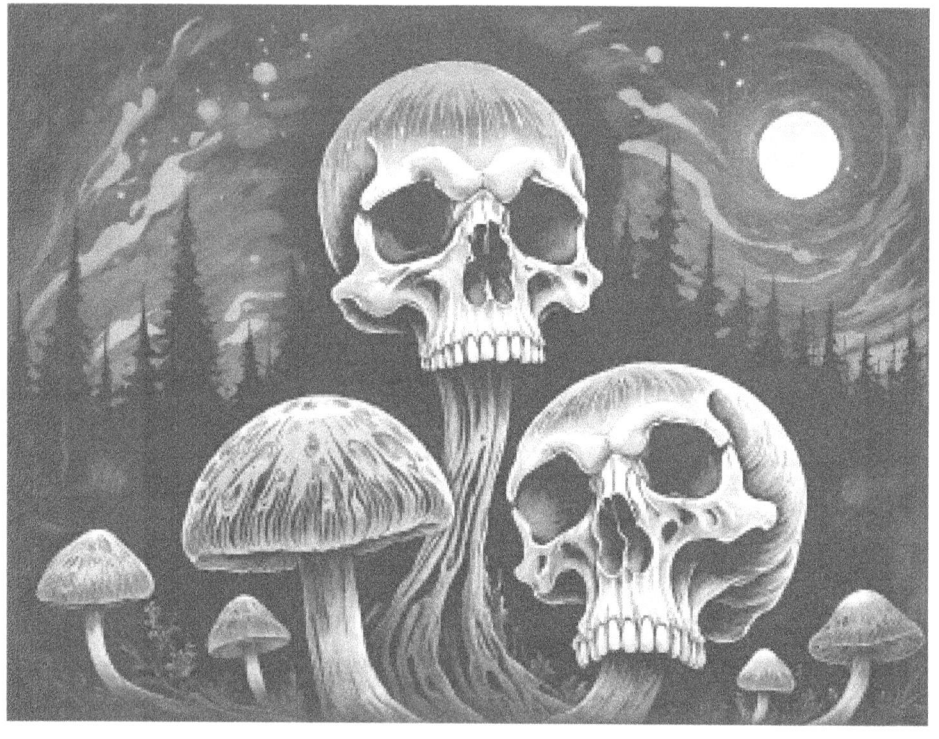

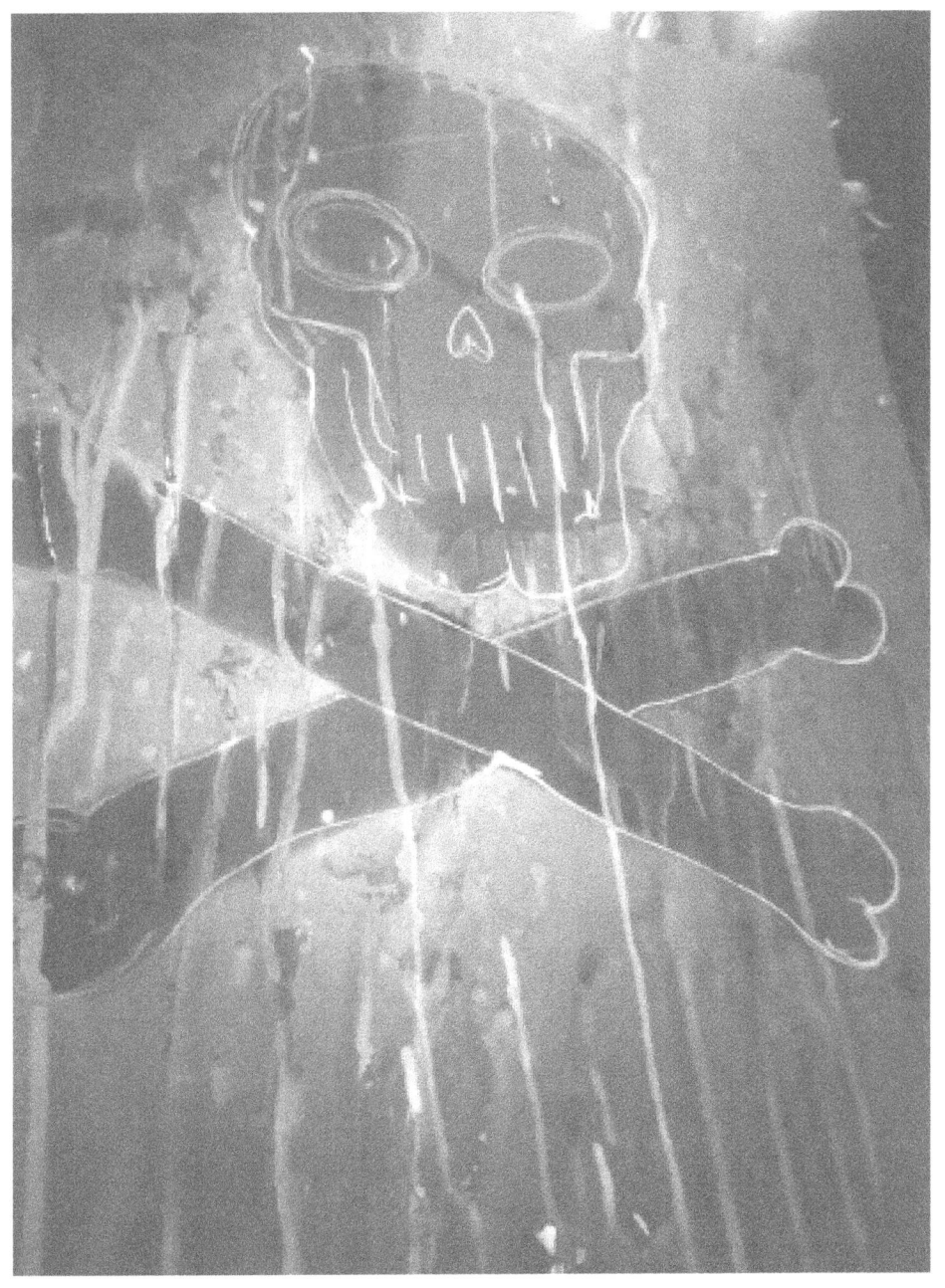

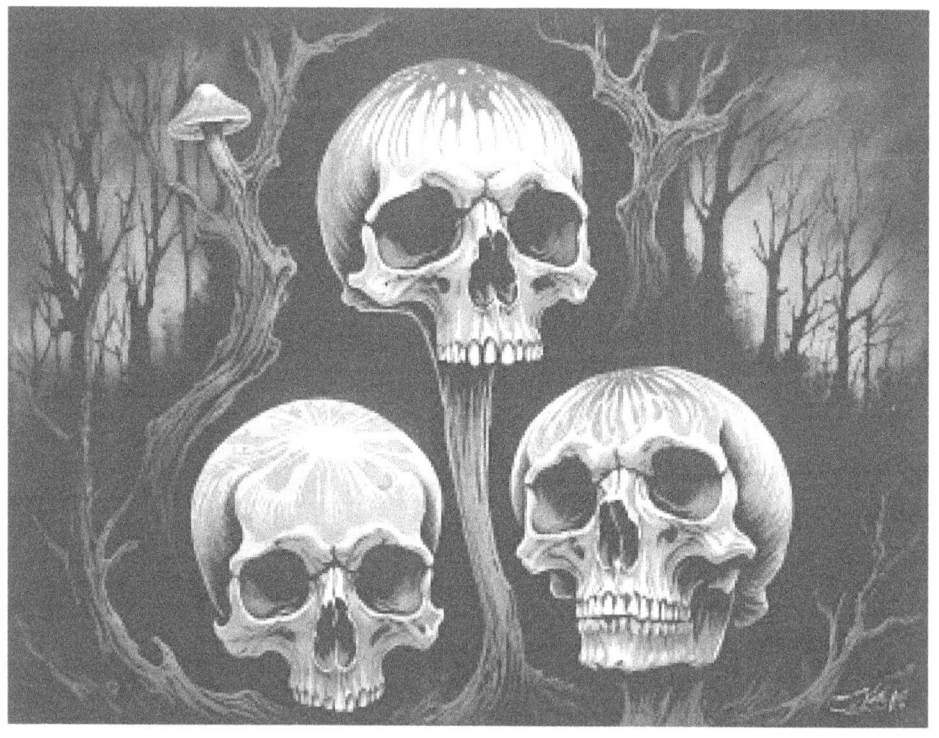

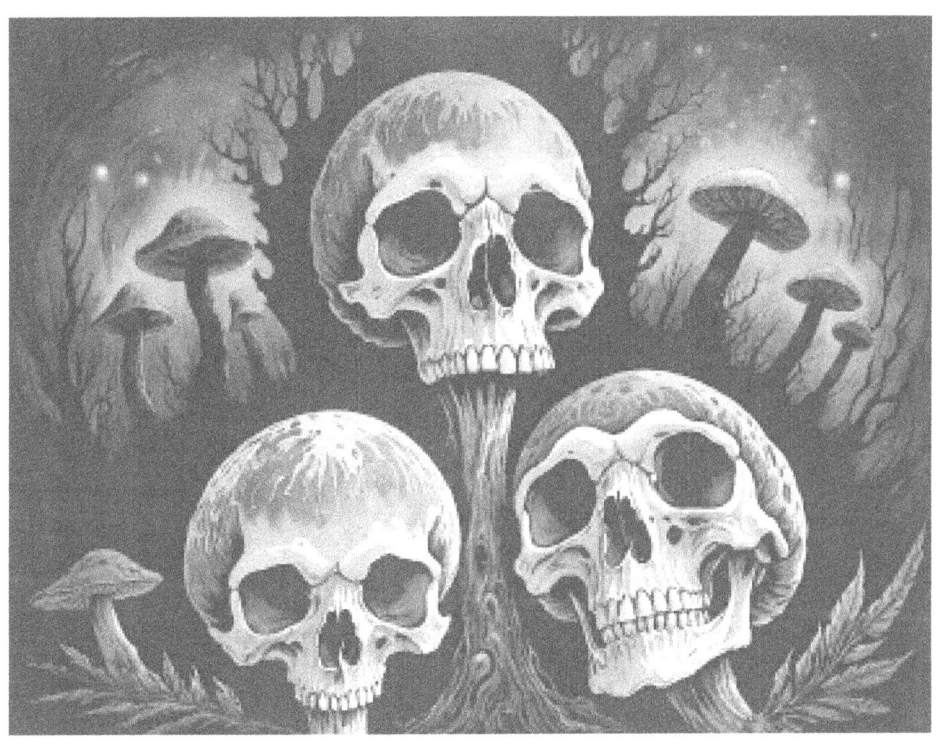

JedidiahDrotar

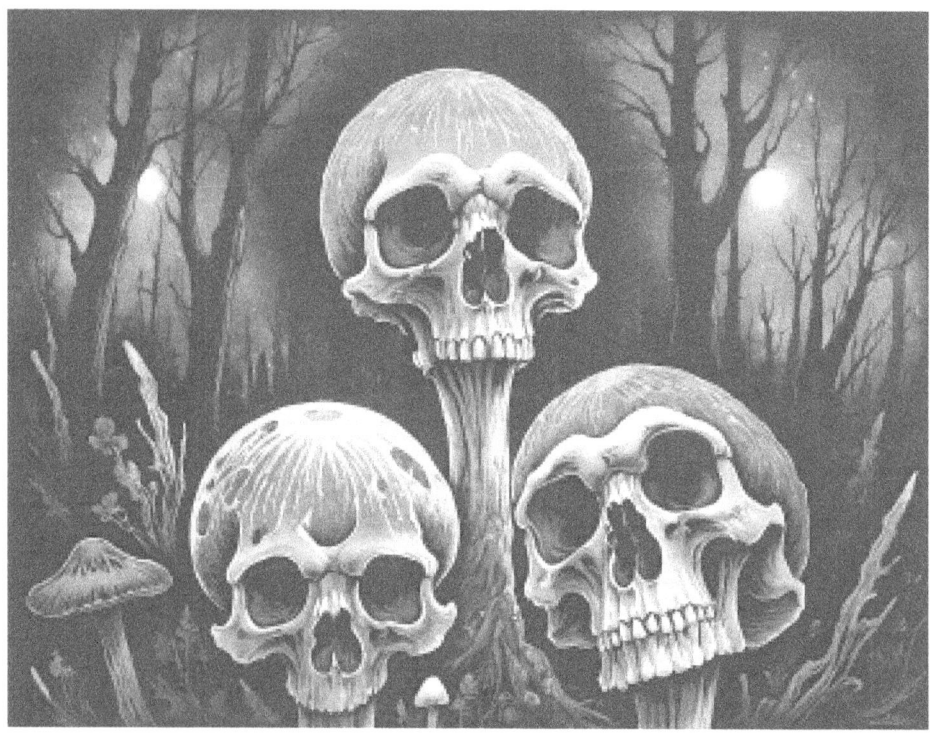

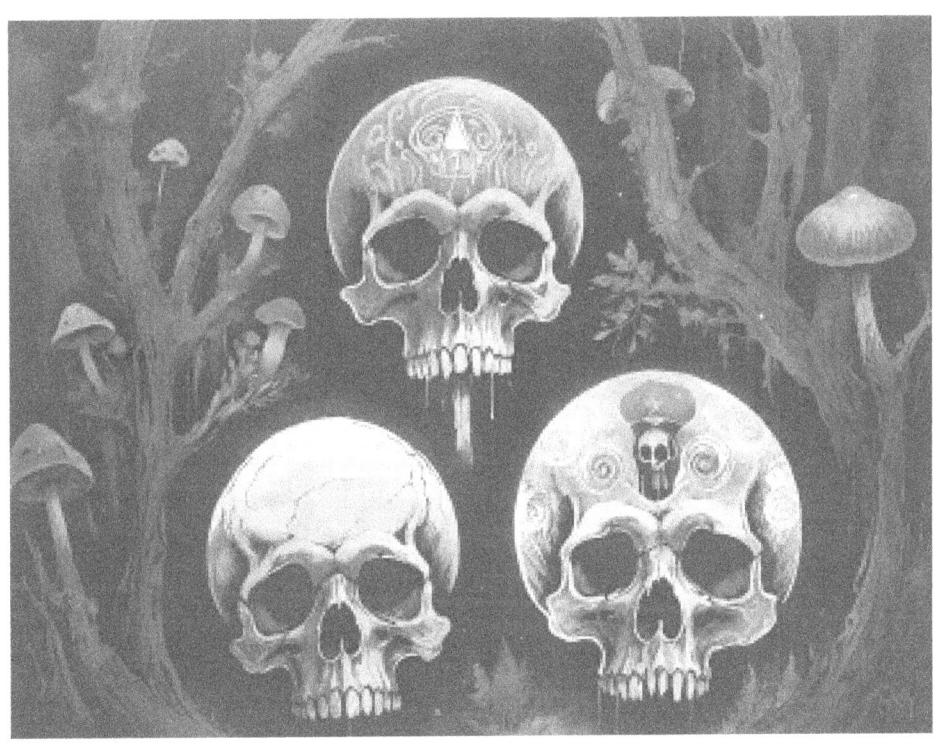

JedidiahDrotar

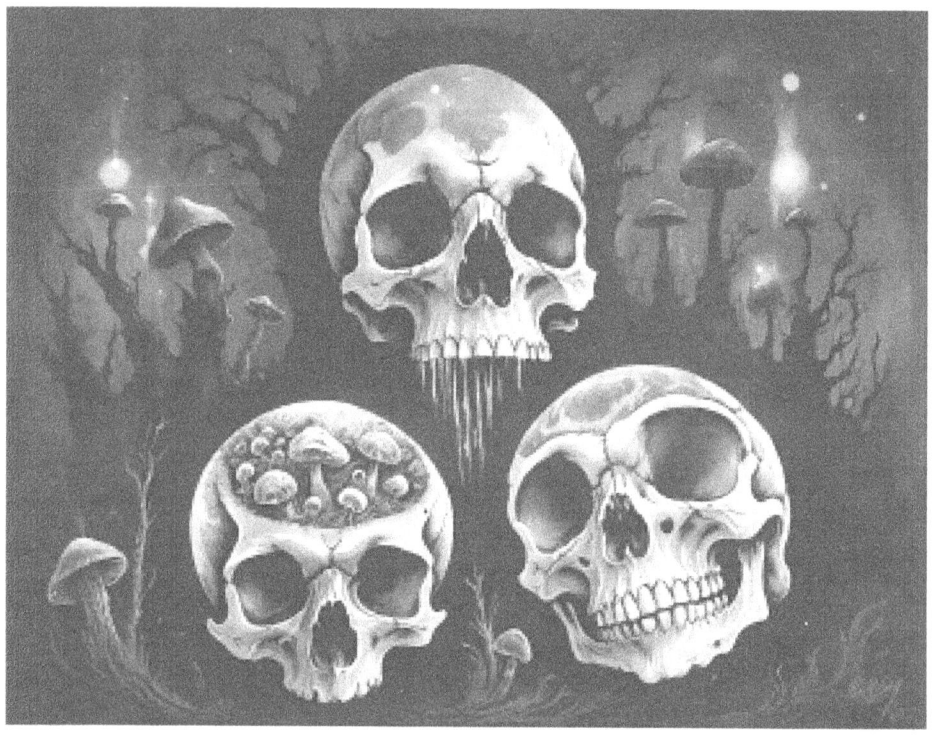

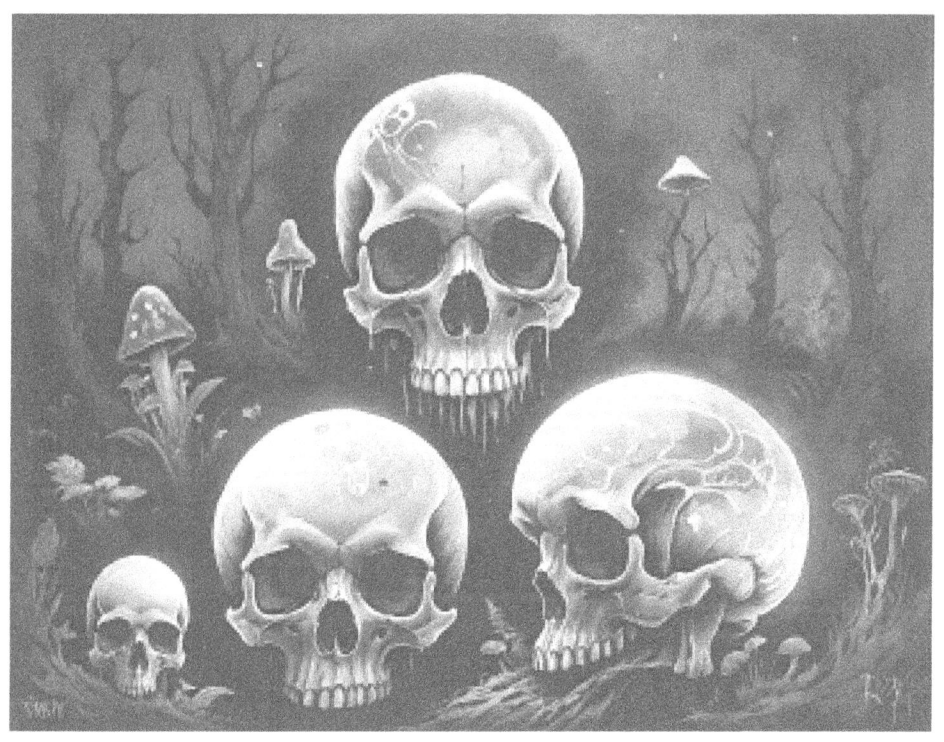

JedidiahDrotar

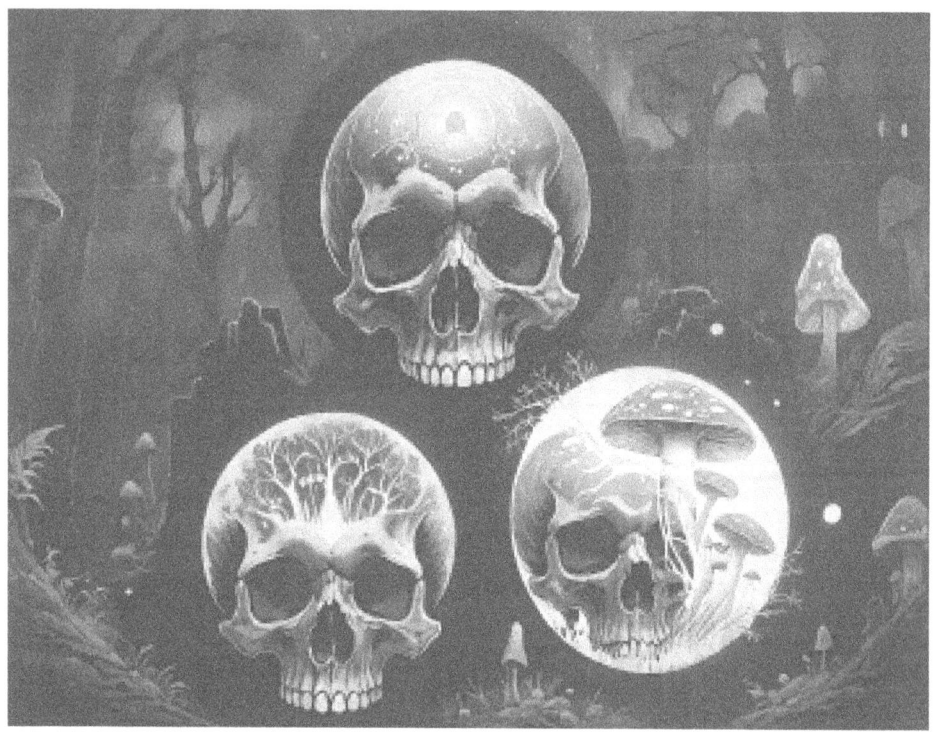

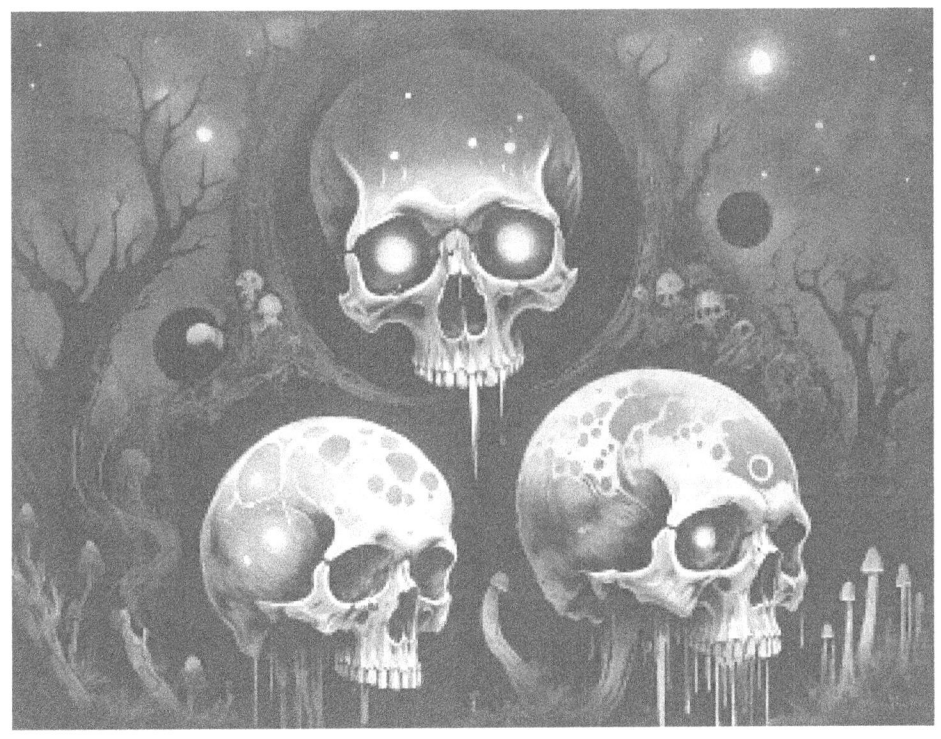

JedidiahDrotar

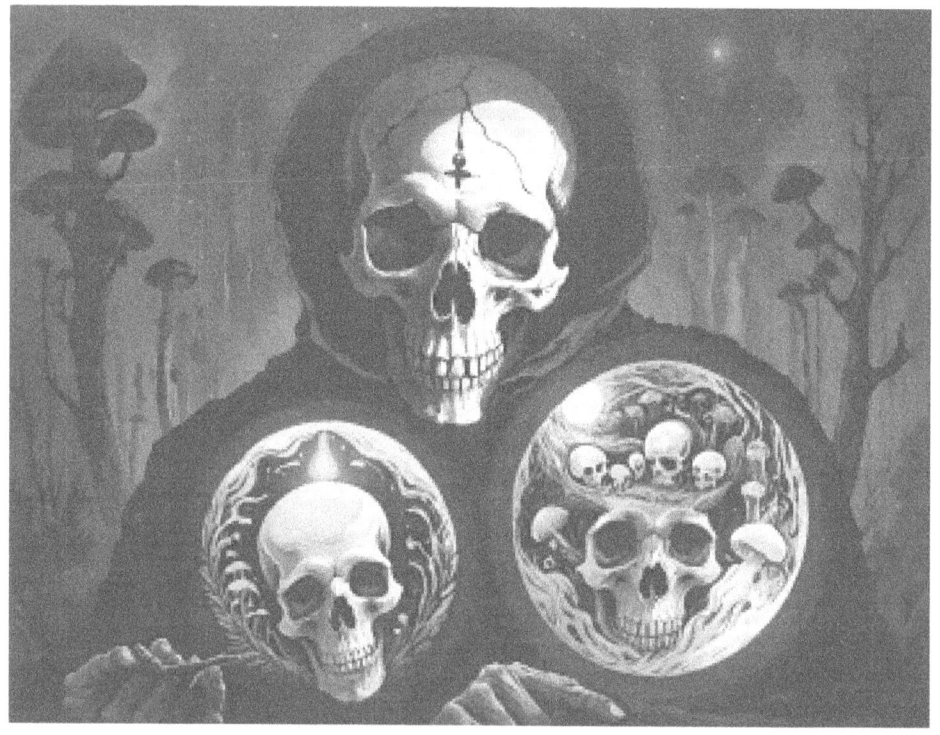

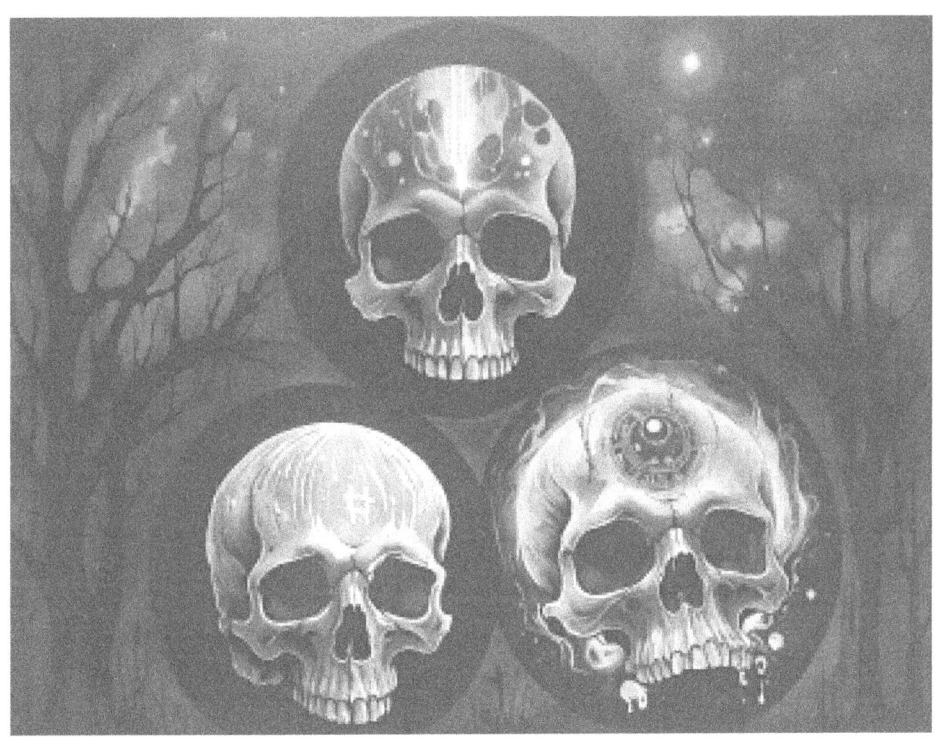

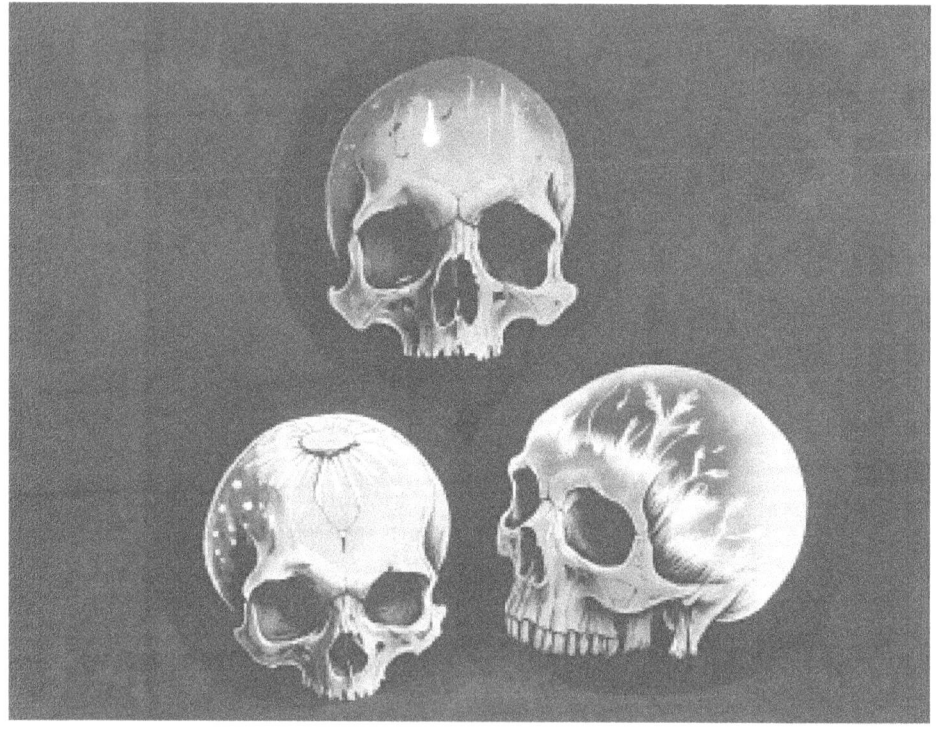

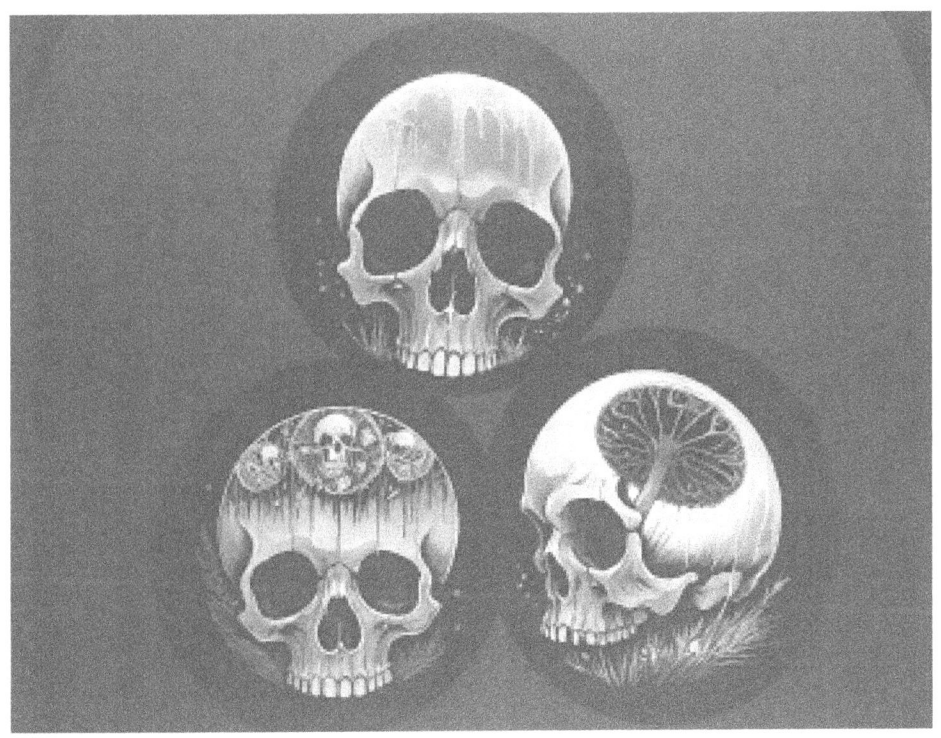

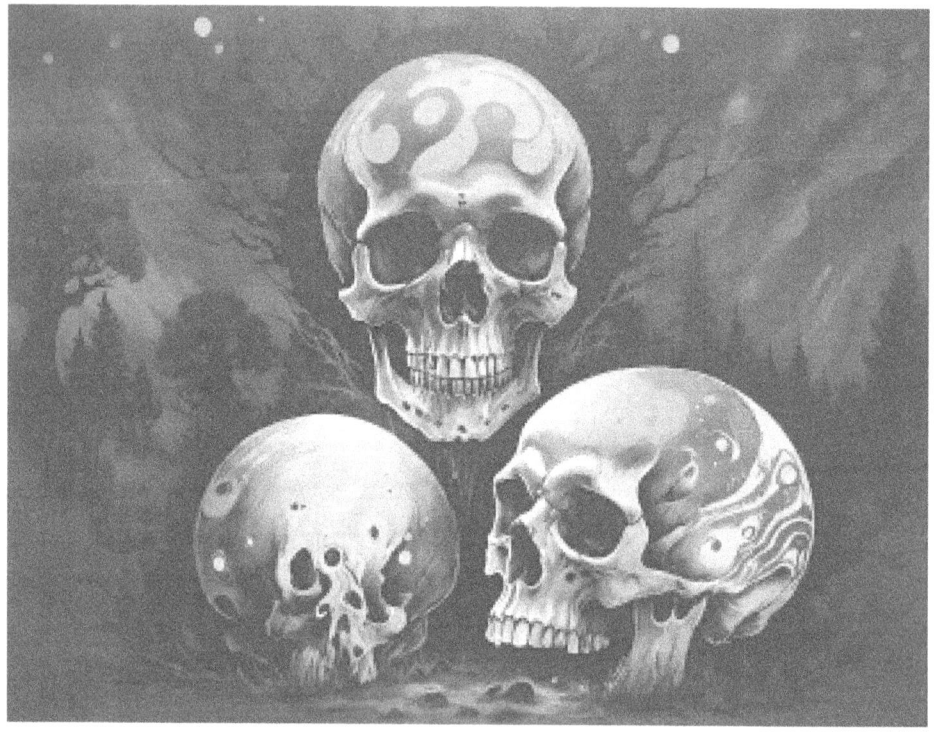

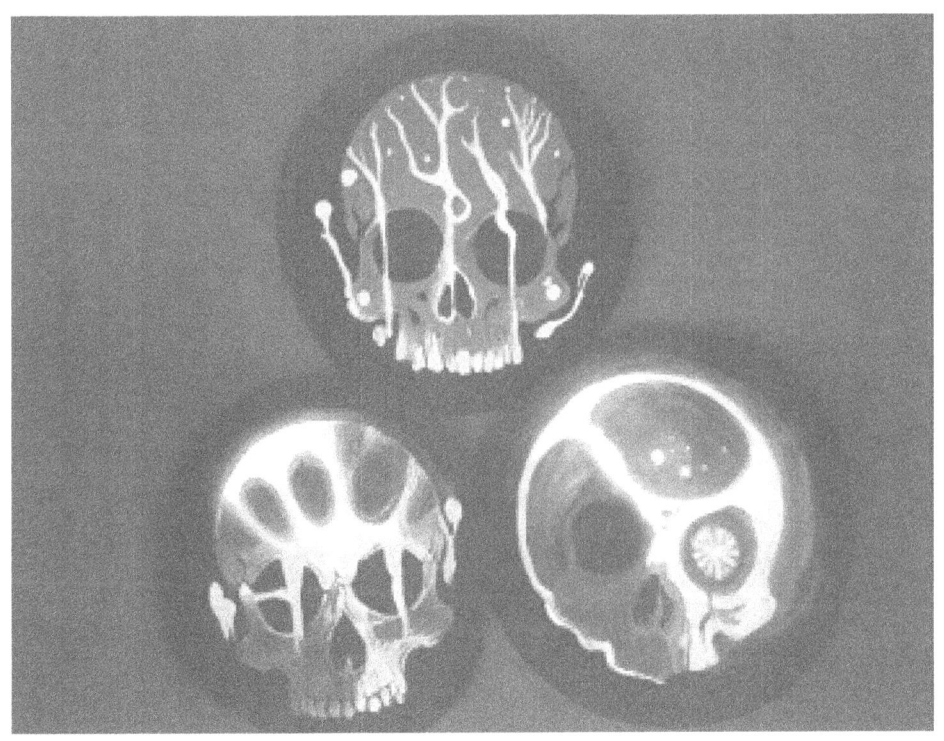

JedidiahDrotar

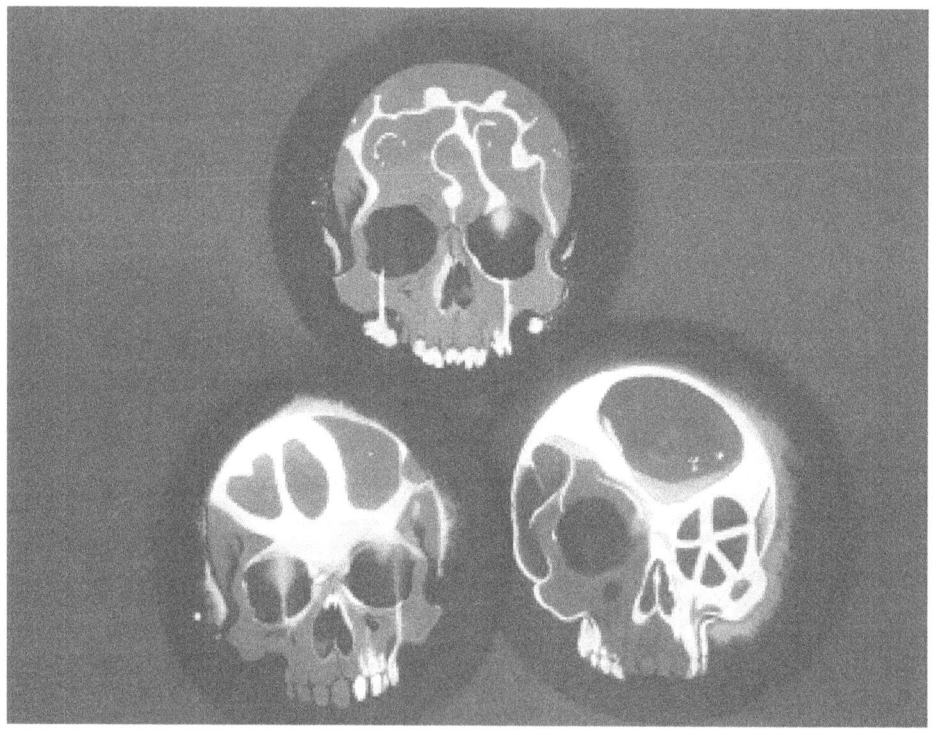

Tripping Hard or Hardly Tripping

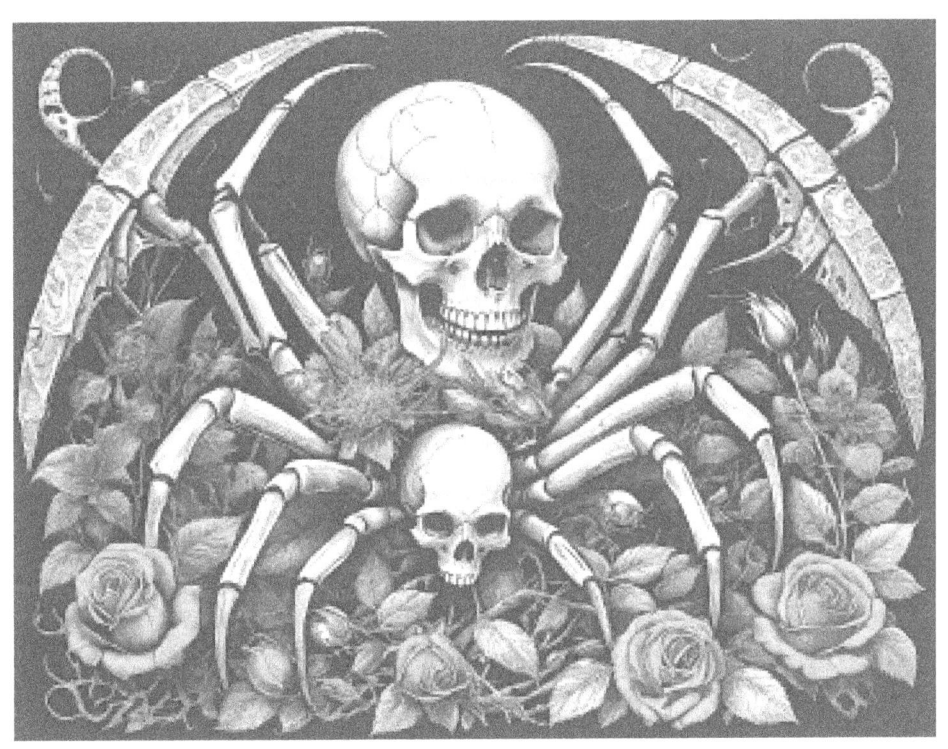

JedidiahDrotar

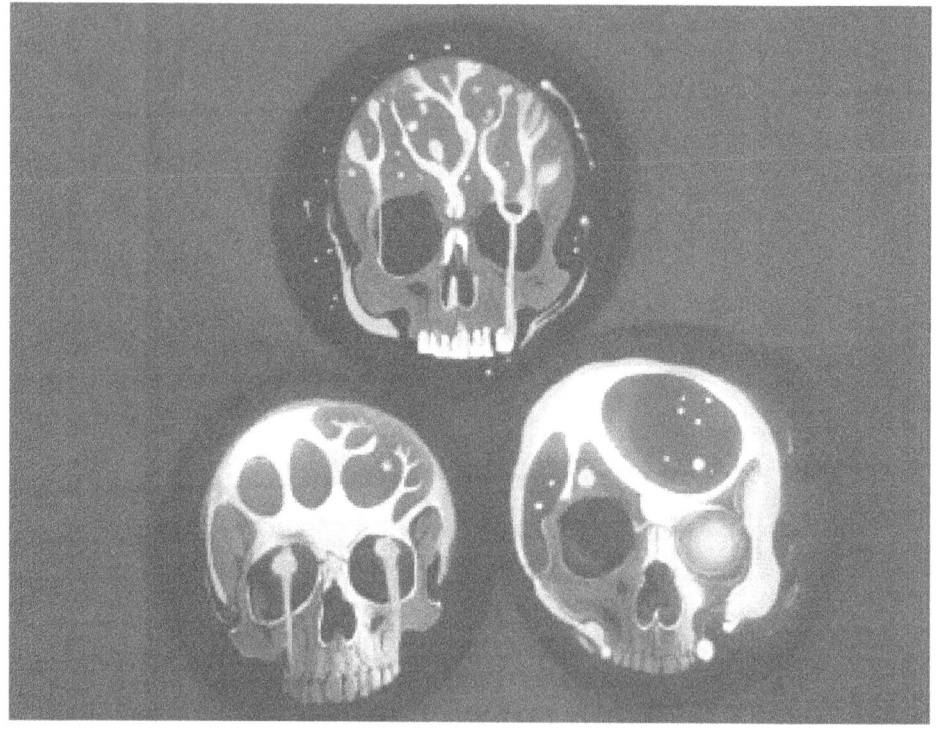

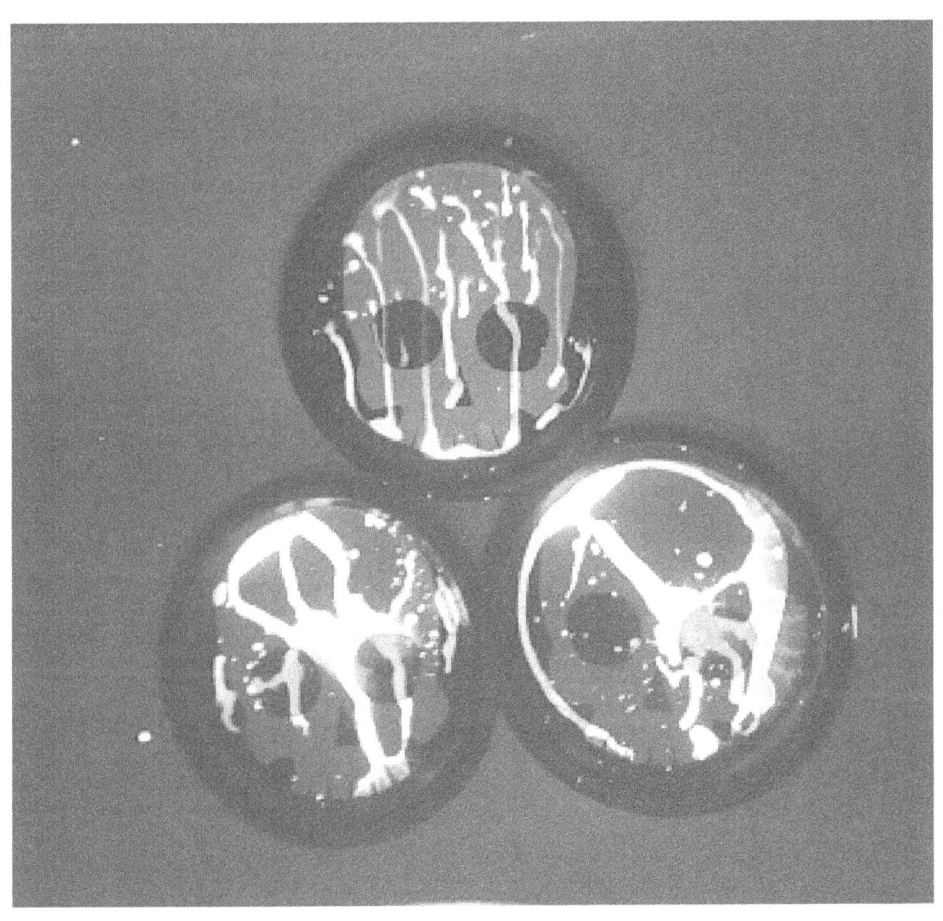

JedidiahDrotar

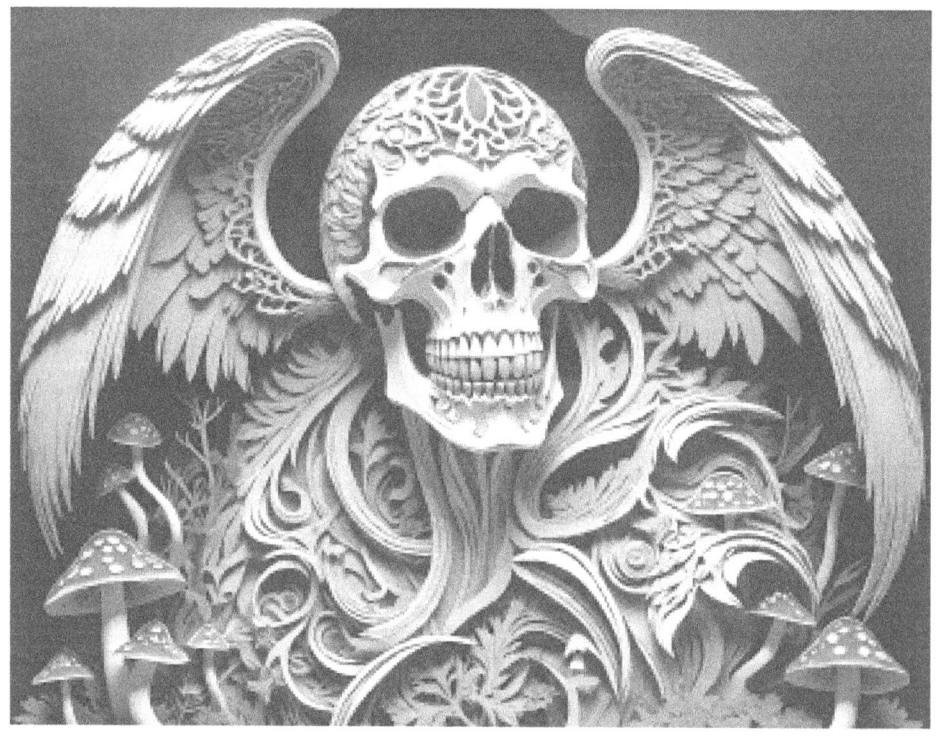

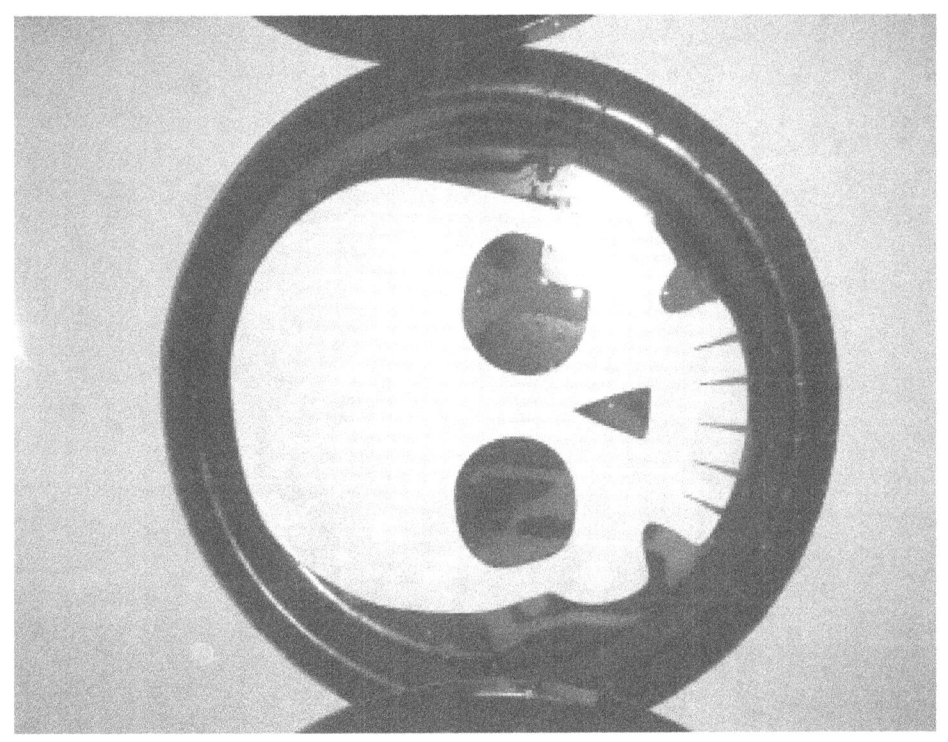

Jedidiah Drotar

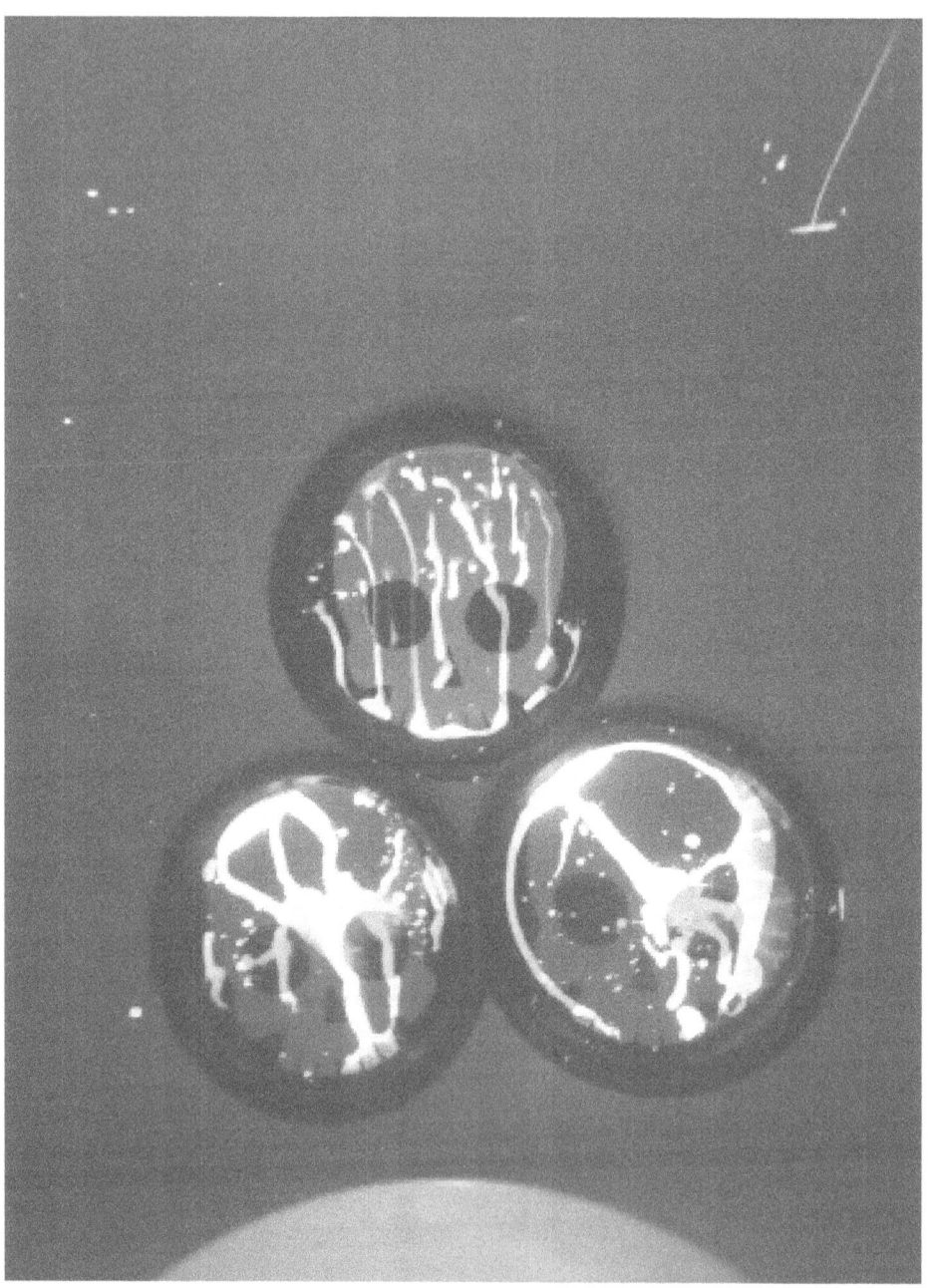

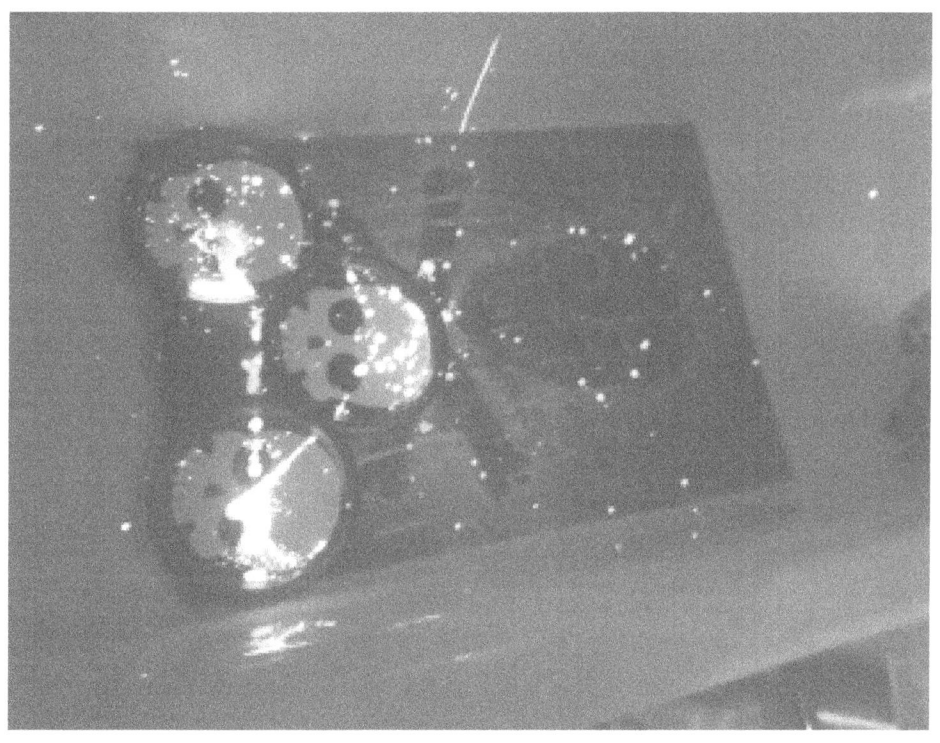

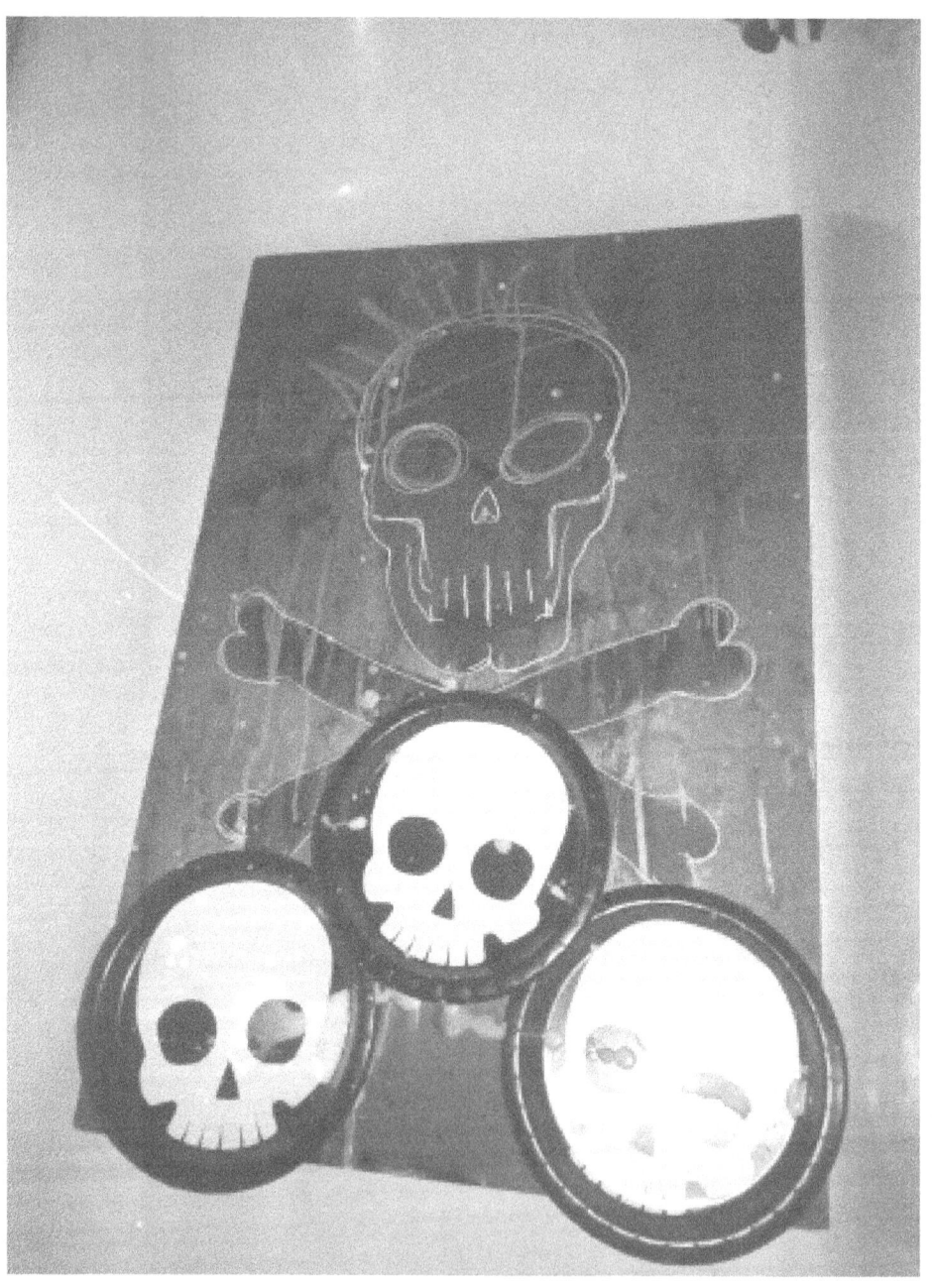

www.ingramcontent.com/pod-product-compliance
Lightning Source LLC
Chambersburg PA
CBHW050327230526
45471CB00005B/2388